DON'T MENTION THE WAR!

A SHAMEFUL EUROPEAN RAIL ADVENTURE

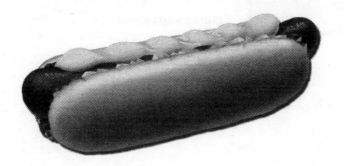

STEWART FERRIS ✳ PAUL BASSETT

summersdale

First published in 1998. Reprinted 2000.

Summersdale Publishers Ltd
46 West Street
Chichester
West Sussex
PO19 1RP
UK

www.summersdale.com

ISBN 1 84024 125 X

Printed and bound in Great Britain.

By the same authors:

Don't Lean Out of the Window!

For E. Doyle

– ACKNOWLEDGEMENTS –

We would like to thank the following people who have not helped with this book in any way: Katia, John Cleese, John 'Fletcher' Tarling, Alastair Williams, Frank Bough, MG Julie, Monsieur Rafting Senior (and Junior), Monsieur Mistral, Uncle Olly, Matt 'Nailgun' Croughan, Kicking Kath, Michael Caine, Monsieur Hair Bear, Thierry & Wonderwoman, Wayne 'Barfer' Daniell, Ginger Spice, Roger, Rodney Dangerfield, Lord Absinthe of Humber, and Mandy.

– CONTENTS –

– FOREWORD –

STEWART

When *Don't Lean Out of the Window!* was published the critics had a field day. The trouble was they were in the wrong field. 'I forgot to read it, actually,' hailed *The Daily Telegraph*. 'Sorry, I think I've lost it. Can you send me another copy?' evaded *The Daily Mail*. A top travel magazine said we were 'funnier than Bill Bryson', but then so is a parking ticket. The review in *The Times* was wildly inaccurate. They called us musicians, for a start, to which Paul takes great offence, and they said we travelled around Europe trying our best to annoy everyone we met. That simply isn't true. I can name at least four people we didn't try to annoy. Well, maybe three.

With such critical acclaim behind us, and with a spare weekend coming up, we couldn't resist writing another book. For obscure technical and grammatical reasons which we don't really understand, some passages in this book could potentially be interpreted as causing offence to certain types of people or individuals, or nations, though this was entirely intentional.

Anyone who doesn't enjoy being insulted, or who lacks a sense of irony due to accident, illness or being American, is strongly advised to go straight to the back of the book which has been designated an Insult-Free Zone. Of those of you who choose to read the whole book, we hereby apologise in advance if you belong to any of the following groups of people: Belgians, Americans, French, Italians, Germans, Welsh, Scottish,

7

Danish, English, and to most other inhabitants of the northern hemisphere. And those in the south. We would also like to apologise specifically to homosexuals, heterosexuals, hermaphrodites, peasants, musicians, fascists, and Americans again.

Finally, we'd like to thank Bruce Forsyth for the birth of the catchphrase as a comedic tool and Rodney Dangerfield for its premature demise.

– Gee, I Can't Get No Respect –

Stewart

'Ladies and gentlemen,' announced the tannoy in our carriage as the train came to a grinding halt, 'this train has caught fire. Please exit the train and walk in single file to the first level crossing where you will be met by a bus. Do not touch the live rail, under any circumstances. I repeat, do not touch the live rail. It's the one in the middle of the track. No, hang on, isn't it the one on the left? I used to know this. Bugger.'

People in the carriage slowly started to gather their belongings.

'Just to keep you informed, ladies and gentlemen,' added the tannoy as I reached for my rucksack, 'it appears that the fire is due to an excessive build-up of friction in the undercarriage.'

'It wasn't me,' said Paul, returning from the toilet.

Alastair packed away his book and looked at the time. It was likely that we would miss our ferry.

'Let's get out before she blows,' he said.

'Before who blows?' I asked.

The sun shone brightly onto the track as we walked alongside it towards the waiting bus. Had the track been newer it would have blinded us with reflected rays, but every photon simply sank without trace into a uniform coating of oxidised brown.

We moved silently in single file, kicking our way through the trackside detritus of crisp packets, Coke cans, jam rags and faeces, all baked to an odourless crisp by the recent heatwave. No human feet had walked this

9

land since the railway had been built – which was the whole point of trains, anyway. I sensed a pioneer spirit amongst our fellow rail travellers that day, a feeling that we were forging a path through a dangerous and untamed jungle. I was right: the outskirts of Portsmouth were upon us.

PAUL

We had not booked a cabin on the ironically named *Pride of Hampshire* for a couple of reasons: we couldn't afford it; and cabins are for girls. Instead, we chose to share an area under the stairs with a few video games and fruit machines. We spread our crap all over the place to deter people from standing on us in order to play SEGA *Virtua Cop*, but within a few minutes, inevitably, a crowd of argumentative, foul-mouthed kids turned up and started fighting over who was going to be first.

'Fuck off, you little bastards,' suggested Alastair, as he climbed into his sleeping bag.

The kids ignored him, of course, and carried on jostling for position at the machines while shouting at the tops of their voices. Predictably, after a few minutes their money ran out and they went off to replenish their coffers, courtesy of their parents. As soon as they had gone, I unplugged the machines at the wall in the hope that the brats would find someone else to annoy. What actually happened was that they waited until about 4 a.m. before returning, switching on the machines and resuming their bickering. By this point we were all too out of it to teach them consideration for others by beating

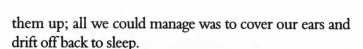
them up; all we could manage was to cover our ears and drift off back to sleep.

The ferry docked at 06:00 local time. This is not a pleasant experience when you've had no sleep due to profane kids. We bundled our crap into our rucksacks and made our way through customs, shuffling in single file through the passport control area. I was last of the three of us and, for some reason, the only one to be singled out for interrogation.

'Where have you come from?' barked the fascist.

'England.' I thought that was pretty obvious, or did they think the ferry had taken a detour via Sierra Leone?

'Where are you going?'

Mmm. Tricky one.

'France,' I replied.

With this harrowing, Gestapo-style interrogation over I was allowed to be on my way to the railway station.

STEWART

The carriage grew dark quite suddenly. I looked out of the train window to find out where all the light had gone: instead of sun-drenched fields there were only high walls blackened by decades of pollution. I realised that we had arrived at the capital of France, a city second only to Amsterdam for prostitutes and second to none for plaster. But once we were off the train and out of the station, the dirt and dark were replaced by the sun's white light shining on a vast expanse of posh architecture. Intricate stone carvings and proud statuettes abounded on every building: historic breasts, ancient bosoms and enormous

11

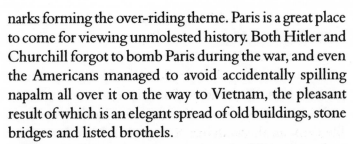

narks forming the over-riding theme. Paris is a great place to come for viewing unmolested history. Both Hitler and Churchill forgot to bomb Paris during the war, and even the Americans managed to avoid accidentally spilling napalm all over it on the way to Vietnam, the pleasant result of which is an elegant spread of old buildings, stone bridges and listed brothels.

We were keen to waste no time in filling ourselves with Parisian culture. Stopping only for a pile of burgers we headed straight for Gare de Lyon where at 11:40 our train would depart for the south coast. We were itching to get moving southwards. Well, we were itching, anyway.

PAUL

The *Train à Grande Vitesse* bound for Marseille travelled so smoothly it was difficult to tell that we were moving at all. This smoothness did not diminish as the speed increased and I wondered why trains couldn't be like this back in Blighty. The difference between British and French tracks, I have since discovered, is that the French apparently have 'superior technology'. This baffles me somewhat. We are not talking about a closely guarded military secret or a tiny piece of micro-circuitry in a laboratory, we're talking about lumps of steel nailed to bits of wood, and not only that but we're talking about something that is found in such abundance that I can't imagine anything easier than travelling to France, looking at the track, ascertaining what is different and copying it. However, this is apparently beyond the capabilities of those responsible for the British railway infrastructure and that's just the way it is.

'*Billets s'il vous plaît*,' said a ticket fascist behind us.

We rummaged around and produced our almost virginal Inter-Rail tickets.

'*Et les reservations?*' he added once he had satisfied himself of the legitimacy of our tickets.

'*Mais il n'y a personne ici*,' protested Stewart. It was hopeless arguing with him though. Monsieur Inspecteur had decided to apply the rules rigidly, and to travel on the TGV you need a reservation even though there were no other passengers in our compartment. This didn't surprise us in the slightest: the French love making up rules which they can then apply, as and when it suits them, to everyone except themselves. Several Francs better off, the fascist was on his way looking for a fourth passenger to separate from his or her money. Feeling pretty pissed off by the whole thing we went back to staring moronically out of the window as the train sped past villages and farms in a blur.

'Fascist!' called Alastair bravely, as soon as the fascist was out of earshot.

★

We had planned to stay with some friends in Provence that night, but our arrangement to meet Charlie and Mandy was, at best, tenuous. When I say 'at best' that is because tenuous is the best arrangement you can ever have to meet with Charlie. Pearl's girlfriend once waited (or wasted) an entire day to meet up with them in Aix-en-Provence. With this sort of reputation in mind, we decided that we should probably phone them to remind them of their promise to meet us in Nice once we arrived. As I was the least athletic, and therefore the most likely

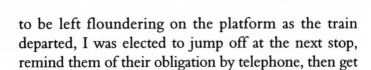

to be left floundering on the platform as the train departed, I was elected to jump off at the next stop, remind them of their obligation by telephone, then get back on the train.

'Go on, Fatty. Run!' enthused Alastair through the train window. My fingers fumbling with the coins, I stuffed a five-Franc piece into the phone and waited. And waited. Then, just as I was about to give up listening to the unanswered phone an answering machine cut in.

'Errr,' it said helpfully, 'are you sure this thing's recording, Honey? Hey, guys, it's Charlie here. If you get this message, then get off at Les Arcs. It's before you get to Nice and we'll meet you there . . . err, be cool!'

I made it back to the train with time to spare and explained that the flimsy plan was now under even greater threat of not happening due to a last minute alteration which Charlie had no way of knowing if we knew about.

★

We arrived in Marseille on time but, having heard some nasty, pointy stories about the city, elected to make a bee-line for the more affluent St Raphaël. The train we caught along the Mediterranean coast was a world apart from that which had brought us from Paris. In a way the trains were representative of the areas they served – the northern TGV was a fast, sleek, efficient object, devoid of any personality while its regional counterpart was grubby, slow, and married to its cousin. But we preferred it. This one at least had internal doors that stayed open while the train was in motion and this in turn kept the multiplicity of odours that was beginning to form from getting too out of hand.

The sights we gawped at longingly as we made our way east at an interminably slow pace were ones of affluence and luxury: tanned people being towed behind speedboats on giant inflatable bananas; young gentlemen on motorcycles with the wind in their hair as they cruised along the beachfront; and some more tanned people being towed behind other speedboats on a variety of fruit-based inflatable vessels. We merely shuffled uncomfortably in our sweaty clothes and tried not to get too jealous.

At St Raphaël we managed to overcome our urges to plunge into the inviting afternoon sea by the infinitely more appealing notion of getting onto another train. This one, the 18:36, went all the way to Nice but stopped at Les Arcs en route, where we hopped off the train and emerged sweating from the underpass that ran beneath the tracks to find ourselves in the station car park. Though there were many cars, we could see no one around who resembled either Charlie or Mandy. We weren't surprised: Charlie was one of the least reliable people imaginable and the whole rendezvous had been arranged via a series of faxed documents, the most recent of which I had sent only a couple of days previously. The fax simply said that we would be arriving in Nice on 14th July and that would he please arrange some supplies of *Herbes de Provence* for recreational use. Then, as a flamboyant touch, I attached a scanned image of a naked woman in a shower. I then sent the document to the number Charlie had given me, blissfully unaware

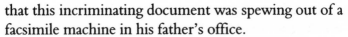

that this incriminating document was spewing out of a facsimile machine in his father's office.

Then, just as we were considering getting on the next train and continuing to Nice, a familiar voice called out from the most distant part of the car park. We hadn't thought to scan the extremities of the station grounds for Charlie's car: Charlie was one of those people who would simply park at the most proximate point to where he wanted to be. This would often mean parking on pavements, humpback bridges, blind corners or private property. In England this behaviour would have made him an arsehole – in France, however, it simply made him one of the locals.

STEWART

Charlie drove his car closer to us, parking on top of a small Citroën in order to save us all a few feet.

'Hey guys, good to see you. Can you all squeeze in the back? Sorry, there's quite a lot of wine in the car. All in? Ok, let's go!'

There used to be a number of hairpin bends between Les Arcs and Vidauban, but Charlie managed to iron most of them out as he piloted us inland. He preferred not to slow down at any point on his journey in order to maintain a constant flow of oxygen onto his smouldering joint. There's nothing more annoying than having to re-light a joint whilst driving.

He took us straight to a restaurant in the town centre. It was an unremarkable establishment, perched on the corner of the main square and surrounded by sprawling terrace tables. The parking spaces in the square were all occupied, so Charlie double parked, completely obstructing two other cars. None of the locals batted an eyelid, though after centuries of in-breeding not many of them had eyelids to bat. This was not a sophisticated area, it seemed: judging from the people in the square the local economy must have thrived upon the sale of flick-knives and bandages.

A skinhead chugged over to us on his moped and addressed Charlie in the local, primitive patois. Charlie mumbled back to him in a jolly fashion, then purchased a bulging envelope from the chap, who promptly rode away again.

'He's been stabbed a couple of times so he doesn't stick around after a deal,' said Charlie. 'He's cheap, though.'

'Nice bloke?' asked Paul.

'Oh yes, thoroughly good egg. Well, not bad for a criminal psychopath, I suppose.'

Several tables had been pushed together in expectation of our arrival. Already seated were Charlie's parents and an American friend of theirs, Roger. He had the appearance of a generic film star, not resembling completely anyone you could name, but possessing an overall look of stardom made up of Robert Redford's blond hair, Johnny Weissmuller's bronzed body, and Ronald Reagan's brain. He didn't say much to us from his end of the table, but already I could sense that this was no bad thing.

During the wait for our first course, the varieties of wine on the table multiplied uncontrollably. At one point Paul had a glass of red wine, a glass of white wine, a glass of rosé, a glass of champagne, a bottle of beer and a glass of water all on the go together. Charlie asked Paul if he had ever tried Muscat, which he said he hadn't. Instantly Charlie ordered a glass of the stuff for Paul to try.

'This is crazy,' said Paul. 'It's blatant debauchery. I haven't finished all these other drinks yet. People keep pouring new drinks for me faster than I can drink the old ones.'

The waiter arrived with Paul's seventh variety of drink.

'What do you think of the Muscat?' asked Charlie.

'I think it sucks,' replied the Wine Critic of the Year.

'Chuck it in the flowers. It doesn't matter,' said Charlie. 'I'll get you some more champagne instead.'

'You're such a hedonist, Charlie,' said Paul.

'I'm a what?'

'A hedonist.'

'No, I'm Catholic. I'm sure I am.'

'No,' explained Paul, ' you're a hedonist. It means you live well, *bon vivant* as the Frogs would say.'

'I'll drink to that!'

Amidst all this profligate excess, I ordered a modest steak. But when it arrived on my plate it was still twitching from the abattoir stun-gun, blood oozing from its many wounds, so I sent it back suggesting they try cooking it a bit. Many sybarite minutes later, when I had almost forgotten about it, the waiter returned with a plate of black cinders, delicately garnished with broccoli. Worse than this, though, at the back of our minds, was the imminence of paying our share of the bill for this Epicurean feast.

This was rather spoiling things. We all had a set menu, the price of which exactly matched the total amount of

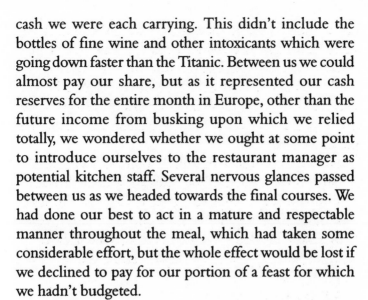

cash we were each carrying. This didn't include the bottles of fine wine and other intoxicants which were going down faster than the Titanic. Between us we could almost pay our share, but as it represented our cash reserves for the entire month in Europe, other than the future income from busking upon which we relied totally, we wondered whether we ought at some point to introduce ourselves to the restaurant manager as potential kitchen staff. Several nervous glances passed between us as we headed towards the final courses. We had done our best to act in a mature and respectable manner throughout the meal, which had taken some considerable effort, but the whole effect would be lost if we declined to pay for our portion of a feast for which we hadn't budgeted.

The waiter finally came over dragging our enormous bill behind him. Charlie's father divided it up evenly, not allowing for the fact that the three of them had been drinking expensive wines on the same bill for some time prior to our arrival. That was our fault for being late.

Into the hat went our last 500 Francs. We were now penniless, too scared to busk in this strange and violent town and so broke that we would have to rely on charity to see us through. I made a point of showing my empty wallet to Alastair and Paul, and they did the same to me in an equally unsubtle manner. Then we started talking about how we would survive until our first busking session tomorrow, and what we would do if it rained.

'I know of a few techniques for effective begging,' said

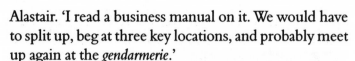
Alastair. 'I read a business manual on it. We would have to split up, beg at three key locations, and probably meet up again at the *gendarmerie*.'

'I could live off my bodily reserves,' suggested Paul.

'That's all very well for you, but what about us? I'm not sticking my fangs into your lard,' I objected. 'Why don't you just sell your body?'

'Who to? A whale blubber factory?' he replied.

Even Roger could have deduced that we didn't have much money. As if by magic, our 500 Francs came back to us before the bill was paid. It was a close thing: fortunately we had had the common sense to dine out with at least two millionaires, otherwise things might have been very different.

PAUL

We left the restaurant and commenced a rambling walk through the narrow streets of the town. Being Bastille Day the general mood was one of conviviality and gaiety.

'This is a special day for the locals,' announced Charlie.

'I know: it's *Quatorze Juillet*!'

'No. Coz the bars are open late.'

'This is France! The bars are always open late by our pathetic standards,' I replied.

'No. Not here.'

I looked at Charlie in confusion.

'Vidauban has a real crime problem,' he explained. 'The police can't control it so they figured the only way to keep crime to an acceptable level is to close all the bars at seven in the evening.'

'Mmmm. I bet that's popular.'

A few moments later we entered a square and it became impossible to move for the sheer number of people. At one end a group of roadies was setting up a stage for what appeared to be an impending concert. Inexplicably, at this point Roger thought he might have something to offer the conversation.

'You guys, I bet you ten bucks I know what the first song the band will play is,' he ventured with an entirely misplaced sense of confidence. I'm not a gambling man but the odds here seemed pretty good.

'What would I want ten bloody Dollars for?' I demanded. 'I wouldn't soil the inside on my wallet with that insidious muck. Give me a wager in a more useful currency and I might reconsider.'

Roger looked confused as if trying to reconcile the fact that there were forms of currency beyond the US Dollar. Charlie leaned over and started to whisper something into my ear but it was soon drowned out by Roger.

'OK. OK. You guys. How would it be if I made it fifty bucks?'

'No. Not. Dollars. Something. Else,' I said, labouring on each word.

Roger entered a familiar state of total confusion. Charlie leaned over again and whispered to me that Roger had been on some kind of programme which had left him particularly susceptible to the effects of alcohol and any other mind altering substance and that it would be best if I laid off him a bit. Remembering the old maxim that if you've not got anything nice to say it's best not to say anything I resolved not to speak to Roger again until absolutely necessary.

STEWART

'One o'clock, three o'clock, two o'clock rock,' sang an emaciated wig stand on the rickety stage, amplified through speakers big enough to convert any hint of musical pitch into a general distorted buzz from which the whole town could benefit. Some might consider this to be adequate entertainment in itself, but our leisure time that evening was further enhanced by the whooshes of fireworks shooting into the sky, by the booms and echoes of sticks of dynamite-sized bangers being let off all over the place by local kids, and by the ambulance sirens arriving to resuscitate what was left of them.

Once enough alcohol had been consumed to make our drivers sufficiently confident of their capabilities, we drove back in two cars. Charlie's parents lived in a beautiful villa in the hills close to Vidauban, with a view from their terrace that stretched for many rugged miles towards the south coast. There to meet us was Bodger, a dog who had been found and rescued by our hosts after a life of abuse and neglect with its previous French owners. Bodger's temperament was surprisingly gentle and serene – clearly he had recovered quickly from the trauma of being introduced to his intellectual match, Roger.

We were shown the various bedrooms, then to the bathrooms, and were strongly invited to make use of such facilities before venturing outside to join the others for more drinks. I dumped my luggage on the enormous oak bed, then wandered into the hall, studying the eighteenth century portraits of the family's debauched ancestors that covered every wall space. Those who weren't too fat to break a horse's back wore hunting apparel, while the rest covered virtually the entire canvasses with their girths. I felt refreshingly skinny as I lay in the bath, staring up at yet another portrait of a fat, dead bloke.

Once we were all clean, we found everyone gathered at the back of the villa, seated on sun-loungers by the swimming pool on a terrace overlooking the small vineyard. Roger was there too, but his acknowledgement of us was minimal, lacking his usual Californian vigour and enthusiasm.

'You guys,' he said softly, before putting his brain into whatever gear it had, 'I was just thinking about some bad news I heard back in the States.'

'What's that?' asked Charlie, with genuine concern.

'Where's that?' I mumbled facetiously to myself.

We all gathered around Roger with sympathetic faces to hear his tale of woe. He took another sip of red wine, and opened his heart to us.

'You guys,' he began again, 'I heard that Rodney Dangerfield is dead.'

There was an uncomfortable silence in which we tried not to snigger. Paul nearly choked. Charlie understood Roger's predicament, but we needed clarification.

'Was he a relative?' I asked.

'I said it was Rodney Dangerfield, you guys. You understand who I mean?' he explained. 'He died last month.' He paused to allow his neurones to catch up with him. 'Gee, haven't you guys seen his pizza ads?'

Charlie admitted to having seen one or two, but I needed to know what on earth he was talking about.

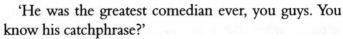

'He was the greatest comedian ever, you guys. You know his catchphrase?'

'Don't keep me in suspense,' I said, boredom oozing from every word.

'No, you guys, that wasn't it. Rodney Dangerfield was a living legend, his catchphrase was "Gee, I can't get no respect".'

'Gee, I can't get no respect?' checked Paul.

'Yes, you guys should check him out.'

'Gee, I can't get no respect?' repeated Paul in his English accent. 'Obviously his death is a major loss to the world of comedy,' he finished, with perhaps more irony than would have been tactful.

'He used to be on the television,' continued Roger, 'every Friday night, you guys, when I was a kid. In the States. "Gee, I can't get no respect" was part of my life, you guys.'

'The dominant part,' I observed.

'Did it have a punchline?' asked Paul.

Roger began to squirm, so Charlie tried to save him.

'It's always sad when your heroes die. What kind of state were you in when you found out?' asked Charlie.

'What state?' checked Roger.

'Yeah.'

'California, of course.'

Just as we were starting to enjoy ourselves, Mandy decided that it was time to stop bullying Roger.

'Who wants wine?' she offered, reaching inside the house to one of the many racks of wine that covered the walls. Grand Crus were devoured like daily milk supplies in this villa, and we demolished a couple of fine bottles immediately.

Occasionally I would listen in on Roger's fond reminiscences of the late comic genius that had shaped his whole personality.

'. . . you guys should see his first movie . . . his early catchphrase was "Gee, thanks mom", which then developed into "Gee, thanks again mom".'

This apparently showed the subtlety of his genius. Roger's genius was pretty subtle, too. None of us spotted it, anyway.

Some months later we discovered that Roger's information was slightly inaccurate to the extent that Rodney Dangerfield was not, much to our eternal relief, dead. Perhaps Mr Dangerfield had forgotten to use his catchphrase one evening and had merely 'died' on stage?

★

The moon rose behind the vines, sending long grapey shadows across us, and turning the black void of the swimming pool into a silvery-black void. Thousands of insects woke up and danced around our candles. Alastair waited for a cloud to cover the moon before finding a discreet bush behind which he could puke up his expensive meal and posh wine, while Paul and I retired to the television to watch German soft porn beamed to us via satellite.

It wasn't midnight yet, and we were working on the assumption that the porn would get harder as the night wore on. This failed to occur, however, despite Charlie's protestations that the quality of the porn was normally top notch. The film we were watching was like a fleshy Benny Hill show, but without the depth and subtlety that characterised the late comic's work and which put him on a pedestal in the Great Hall of Comedians, between Rodney Dangerfield and the emergency exit. The gist of the film was that fat German men were bouncing up and down on top of large-breasted German women as if they were trampolines.

Paul was busily taking notes when Mandy stuck her head round the corner to remind Charlie that this was not sufficiently edifying for him.

'Charlie didn't want to watch it,' I protested on his behalf. 'We made him do it.'

'They said they would throw my best hat into the swimming pool if I didn't watch German pornography with them,' said Charlie.

'That's right,' added Paul. 'The baseball cap would have been the first to go.'

'Go to bed, little boys,' ordered Mandy.

– ROUTE NAPOLEON –

PAUL

Charlie turned the car down a dusty track and past a couple of signs saying *'Propriété Privée'* – still, that didn't matter: from what I'd seen on the news at home the French seemed very adept at ignoring laws they didn't much like the sound of and, as they say, when in Rome . . .

We parked up underneath a suitably shady tree and threw all our valuables in the boot; that would be sure to thwart any thieves that came prowling while we were away. Charlie led the way along a path and then through a barbed wire fence.

'Is this OK?' said Alastair, 'I mean look at all these signs. They mean no entry, right?'

'Everybody comes here,' reassured Mandy.

'Well, that's all right then,' muttered Alastair under his breath.

As we made our way down the bank it became apparent to us that the French authorities had been most pragmatic in the deployment of their warning signs. Right at the entrance by the main road was the sign that said 'Private Property. Entry Forbidden'. They had rightly assumed that people would ignore that. Then, by the barbed-wire fence was another that read 'Private grounds belonging to EDF (Electricité de France). Danger of death. Keep out.' Then, halfway down the slope to the river at the bottom was a sign that read something along the lines of 'Sudden and unpredictable changes in water levels will occur due to the sluices at the hydro-electric plant upstream. Extreme danger, everything is forbidden, blah

blah, etc. etc.'. Then, knowing that the public normally reads signs and then simply assumes that the signs apply to everybody but them, EDF had erected a final sign at the water's edge. Its pole had weed and shreds of plastic bag wrapped around it and was listing slightly downstream. It had obviously spent a significant part of its existence underwater. The sign read 'This place is very dangerous. If you have got this far it is because you have ignored all the previous signs. If you do swim here it is at your own risk and EDF will bear no liability at all if you are killed.'

'OK! Last one in's an American!' shouted Charlie as he threw himself sideways into the water. I dipped my foot into the water like a girl: it was so cold I could not believe that it could still be fluid. I climbed back up the bank and from there onto a jutting piece of rock that rose up from the middle of the river like a small cliff. I squatted on my haunches surveying the unattractive proposition of immersing myself in the glacial flow. The sun was beating its warm rays on my back as if to say, 'Stay here. It's really nasty in the water'. However, I had already lost face by still being dry while Charlie was floundering around like a walrus in the water. The thought of implicitly becoming an American was too much for me, though, so – steeling myself against the impending thermal shock – I jumped the twenty or so feet from the rock into the waters below.

As I plunged beneath the surface I felt like a new horseshoe must as it is plucked from the forge and dunked into the quenching bath. Every nerve ending seemed to be screaming 'You utter bastard!' as they rapidly tried to adjust to the difference in temperature. My head broke back through the surface as I gasped for breath, more from shock than oxygen deprivation.

'You all right, mate?' shouted Alastair from on top of the rock.

'Yeah, fine,' I lied.

'You've hurt yourself,' added Stewart.

'Eh?'

'You've got blood pissing out of your nose!'

I wiped the back of my hand over my top lip. Sure enough there was the orange colour of diluted blood. I dragged myself back out of the water and sat on the rock.

'Must have been the change in temperature,' declared Alastair, our undergraduate in chiropody and stand-in doctor.

Once we had become as accustomed as possible to the icy waters we decided to explore upstream a little. The landscape was inspirational. Apart from the occasional sign warning of a multiplicity of dangers there was no indication that the area had ever been touched by humans. At one point we even found a waterfall where a trickle of water fell from about fifty feet up. To stand in it was like taking a warm shower . . . though bearing in mind this warmth was relative to the water we were swimming in, its temperature was probably around the same temperature as the Serpentine in Hyde Park on Christmas Day.

A little while later we were all sitting on the jutting rock basking and smoking when Charlie remembered that he had brought a plaything with him to amuse us.

'Check this out guys!' Charlie held up an orange package about the size of a life jacket. 'It's a life jacket. Cool, huh?'

'Wouldn't that be more gainfully located in some form of transport?' ventured Stewart. 'Maybe the aeroplane that it came from?'

'I got it on a New York Air flight last year,' explained Charlie. 'They really pissed me off so I swiped it to get even.'

'Really? What did they do to deserve that?' I asked, intrigued.

'They just refused to serve me any more wine. They said that if I'd already thrown up twice then I'd probably had enough.'

'Ah right. Yeah, bang out of order that was,' I said, trying to sound as if I meant it.

'Anyway, does any of you want to try it out?'

For some reason it was decided that it should be me to execute the experiment. I pulled the vest over my head, tied the cord around my waist as I had seen demonstrated on every flight I had ever been on, and slipped back into the water.

'Let it off underwater,' urged Alastair who was around that time being inspired by the bravery and courageous acts recounted in Wilbur Smith novels. I swam down around six feet, wedged myself between two submerged rocks to prevent my buoyant love-handles from lifting me to the surface, and turned to face the surface. I could see four faces peering through the rippled surface. The faces looked distorted and twisted but I suppose one should blame the parents, really. Realising that I was running short on oxygen I decided that I ought to inflate the jacket. In an instant I had pulled the tab and was bobbing around on the surface with my little red marker light blinking away, barely noticeable in the midday sun. Two things became apparent once I had inflated the jacket. Firstly, that it was absolutely impossible to turn onto one's front to climb out of the water. Thinking about this, it does not seem to be a particularly beneficial feature of an item of safety equipment. I can only imagine the number of shipwrecked passengers who have been unable to climb into a waiting lifeboat because of the way that these jackets immediately turn one onto one's back. Secondly, that having been manhandled out of the river by my four-man strong support team there was no obvious way of getting the jacket off – the vest had inflated so thoroughly that the neck hole was now too tight around my neck to be lifted over my head. In the end, we had to burn a hole in it with a cigarette lighter.

★

Back at the house, Charlie's mum had prepared a fantastic spread of food for lunch before we ventured north towards Castellane. Charlie's old dear was an absolute master in the art of cuisine: a fact borne out by the sheer number of wine bottles she had in the kitchen purely for cooking purposes. This collection of a dozen or so half-empty bottles comprised vintages which we three would happily have served at table, had we been sophisticated enough to eat at a table. The meal of pasta, salad and, surprise surprise, wine, was served on the terrace, where we were joined, to our horror, by a local Gendarme. Guilty glances flew like arrows between us.

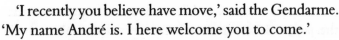
'I recently you believe have move,' said the Gendarme. 'My name André is. I here welcome you to come.'

I resisted the temptation to snigger, realising that my French probably sounded just as bad to one of the natives.

'That's very kind,' replied Charlie's mother in French. 'Would you care to join us for lunch?'

What a bloody cheek, I thought. How dare he scare us shitless with a social visit? It was completely uncalled for. Here we were, miles away from anywhere, stuck on a hilltop surrounded by vineyards and rocky terrain, from where we should be allowed to get on with whatever dubious or illegal pastimes we wanted to without living in fear of friendly visits from the local fuzz. How would the French fascists feel if I went down to their police station canteen and helped myself to their croque monsieurs and Oranginas in the name of community relations? They'd put me away.

Charlie produced a bottle of Pimms halfway through the meal, and poured it into a large jug with ice, lemonade and borage. It was more refreshing than red wine, and proved popular with the Gendarme who had never tasted it before. He poured himself a tall glass of the stuff, took a sniff, then downed it in one.

'I refreshed now,' he declared, leaning back in his chair. He squirmed because his gun was digging in to his side, so he pulled it roughly out of its holster and plonked it on a little table next to the cheeses. Charlie topped up his glass with another large serving of Pimms, dripping a little from the jug onto the gun as he leaned over. André drank a couple more glasses during the meal, and by the time we had finished he was so *soûl* out of his mind that we had come to regard him not just as a policeman, but almost as a fellow human being. He looked at his watch, failed to focus his eyes sufficiently to deduce the time, but said that he ought to get back on duty anyway.

We carried on with dessert, much relieved that the friendly fascist was gone, but it was some moments before anyone noticed that there was still a gun on the table.

'Is that yours?' Stewart asked Charlie.

'No. I thought it must be yours,' he replied.

I heard the police car's engine running, behind the villa, then it stopped. André got out and staggered back round to our terrace.

'My forget I gun,' he said, bumping against the table as he picked up his pistol. 'Very apologise.'

'You'd forget your brain if you had one,' I said, quickly and quietly.

'Thank you bye,' said André, heading back to his car. This time the engine started and revved loudly until the car moved away down the gravel track towards the road.

'That was a close one, eh, Fingers?' Alastair whispered to me.

'Yeah, Knuckles. Where did you stash the loot?' I replied.

'Up my arse.'

The tension of the meal dissipated into the warm air as soon as the Gendarme was gone. We returned to our usual topics of conversation: the local drug dealers, alcohol and sex, all discussed at length over large glasses of red wine. But we had hardly got down to the sex bit when the deepset French features of André poked their irritating way around the corner yet again. He was sweating profusely, white-faced and rubbing his left shoulder like it was his groin.

'André, sit down, what's happened?' asked Charlie's mother.

It was a fact that I hadn't heard his car arrive this time. It was also a fact that he appeared to be in shock. These two facts swam around independently in my brain for a second or two, looking for each other. Then they met. An enormous smile broadened across my face as I realised he had crashed his police car because we had got him pissed on Pimms. So he was human, after all.

★

When André's car had been dragged out of the ditch by a discreet farmer who recognised a good opportunity for blackmail when he saw one, it was time for us to think about getting ourselves up to Castellane in time to set up our tent for the night. Alastair had mentioned during the meal that he had written a recipe book, so Charlie's mother decided to give him a copper colander as a buggering-off present to assist with the preparation of the all the complex and sophisticated meals of dry bread and chocolate biscuits that we would be preparing during our travels. A car was made available to us by Charlie's father, who foolishly gave him the keys to the Renault again. He then said goodbye and retired to his study to do some 'work' – more arduous wine tasting, no doubt.

With all five of us and all of our assorted crap loaded into the large hatchback, we tore off up the unmade track at a speed that would make most car owners wince. Still, cars, as far as Charlie was concerned, were things that

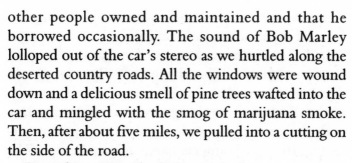

other people owned and maintained and that he borrowed occasionally. The sound of Bob Marley lolloped out of the car's stereo as we hurtled along the deserted country roads. All the windows were wound down and a delicious smell of pine trees wafted into the car and mingled with the smog of marijuana smoke. Then, after about five miles, we pulled into a cutting on the side of the road.

'Everything OK, Charlie?' we asked.

'I think I'm too stoned to drive. I keep seeing things that aren't there,' he confessed.

'Like speed limit signs?' jibed Stewart, in a way that would have had us walking the remaining fifty miles were anyone else driving.

'Can you drive, Honey?' he asked Mandy.

'I've had too much to drink. Paul's a good driver,' she suggested, conveniently forgetting about the time I destroyed my robustly built Volkswagen Golf by driving it into the rear of a stationary Honda Prelude while searching for a cigarette lighter in the passenger footwell.

Cautiously, then, I engaged first gear and shakily continued the journey north. Although I had driven on the right before on a few occasions, I had never done so in a left hand drive car and so every time I went to change gear I opened the window with my (often neglected) left hand. Once I had mastered this small anomaly we continued at a sedate pace up the Route Napoleon towards Castellane. Why Napoleon was looking for a campsite near Castellane isn't clear, and why he should be honoured for it I have no idea. If it's a military

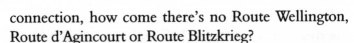

connection, how come there's no Route Wellington, Route d'Agincourt or Route Blitzkrieg?

In the late afternoon, we entered the gates of Camping Frederic Mistral. The site was really a large, old farmhouse set in what must have once been an immense garden. Sometime, way before we ever sullied Castellane with our presence, the gardens had given way to a never-ending stream of campers from all over Europe. The site was run by a couple who we suspected were in their early sixties: he a short but very powerfully built man with an ever-lasting cigarillo protruding from under his sun hat; she a typical French peasant woman with a face like a sultana and wearing a nylon overall. We never made any attempt to find out their names as we had already decided that his name was Frederic Mistral and that she must therefore be Madame Mistral. We were probably wrong about this supposition as the road on which the site was situated was also called Rue Frederic Mistral.

'Vous voulez un emplacement pour trois personnes?' enquired Madame Mistral. She drew her breath over the remains of her teeth and tutted to herself as if this request was unreasonable in some way.

'Errrr, ouai?' I tried to look over her shoulder to see what was written in her pocket book she was referring to. What if it was a blacklist of unsavoury campers in which, through no fault of our own (except for the time we incited civil unrest at Camp du Verdon, and the time we broke his fence, and the time . . . etc) we had been included? It wasn't, of course; she was merely trying to work out where she could accommodate us.

'*Desolé. Complet!*'

'She says they're full, lads,' I explained to the others.

'Couldn't she squeeze us in between those pear trees behind the barn?' suggested Alastair.

I asked Madame Mistral and in turn she looked at me as if I were mad. In the end we had to show her where we meant. She still thought we were mad but agreed to let us pitch our tent on the windfall fruit and tangled roots of the trees.

STEWART

Charlie and Mandy left us to set up our excuse for a tent while they wandered into town to read the menus of restaurants at which they could afford to eat but which we couldn't, and to argue over whether they should compromise their taste buds by eating foods priced at the group's lowest common budgetary denominator so that we could all eat at the same table. We just fancied a pizza.

It took us no more than five minutes to transform the tent from a floppy rag to a proud erection, even with Madame Mistral's off-putting sultana face glaring at us from her doorway. We then met up with Charlie and Mandy at a pizzeria where Jean-Noel served us with the biggest, juiciest, eggiest and most garlicky pizzas ever produced. He was the proprietor of La Main A La Pâte, which roughly translates as The Chef Puts His Dirty Hands In Your Dinner, but he produced the best pizzas on the planet. The only words he ever spoke to us were '*En forme?*', accompanied by a simulated guitar strumming motion. It was a bizarre way to communicate,

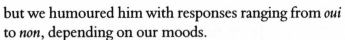

but we humoured him with responses ranging from *oui* to *non*, depending on our moods.

The tables on the street around us were full by the time we had finished our pizzas, so it was time to earn some money to pay for them. The first song we played was a simplified and edited version of an already simple song, *Bye Bye Love*. It went down well because we all managed somehow to play it in the same key and to finish within a bar of each other (Paul ended up in Jo-Jo's and we finished in La Taverne). Mm, bad joke. Sorry.

Charlie and Mandy drank more wine in order postpone the delivery of the bill to our table, and thus to give us enough time to bash out three or four more songs and then collect payment from the audience. I picked up my hat and nervously tackled the straggly crowd that had assembled, while Alastair zoomed in on the seated audience, earning significantly more than me because his victims couldn't run away. We spread the loot across the table and counted it: there was enough for our bill plus some change to donate to our favourite charity, probably Jo-Jo's.

'*En forme?*' called Jean-Noel, striding over to our table.

'*Oui*,' I decided to answer.

I proffered a handful of coins in his direction, but he smiled and pushed them away.

'*Non, non*, is free *pour les musiciens!*' he said, chirpily. I suspected he may have been at the olive oil again. He disappeared briefly indoors then re-emerged with a bottle of his home-brewed napalm that was a big as a child, a bottle-shaped one. '*Vous voulez une aperitif?*'

In this context I think he was asking if we would like to set ourselves on fire, but without waiting for an answer he poured out five little glasses of the misty liquid. Inside the bottle I could see a substantial amount of foliage hovering close to the bottom: there was a small tree, a number of free-floating chillies, and an old bicycle. This stuff had been brewed to perfection.

I lifted the glass close to my nose, taking care not to ignite it from the burning candle on the table. Before I had taken as much as a sniff, most of the delicate hairs on the inside of my nostril instantly evaporated, and those that were left were bleached white.

'Down in one!' shouted Paul.

The five of us raised our glasses and poured the burning liquid down our throats. I felt its heat spreading into my stomach, neck and head, setting off fire extinguishers in my eyes and pressure release valves in my ears. I took several deep breaths, wiped my eyes, and looked around for any survivors. We were all moist-eyed, trying desperately not to do anything embarrassing like die.

'I think we'd better get going, Charlie,' said Mandy. 'We've got a long drive home tonight.'

'Why don't you stay in Castellane and go back tomorrow?' I asked.

'Yes, why don't we, Charlie?'

'Gee, Honey, I'd love to but my father will be wanting the car in the morning.'

'*En forme?*' asked Jean-Noel yet again as he breezed up to our table.

'*Non,*' I answered this time, pointing to my throat.

He knew what the problem was and how to cure it. Quicker than we could say 'drink-drive limit' he had refilled our little glasses with more of his high octane aviation fuel and was hovering over us, applying psychological pressure not to let him down. I picked up the glass and tried to move it close to my unwilling throat with a shaking arm. The others managed to drink theirs in one shot, so despite my body's protestations I raised it to my mouth and poured it in.

Two Charlies and three Mandys either shook my hand or kissed goodbye at that point, or so I guessed. I knew someone was leaving, but my perception of events was now filtered through such a strong alcoholic haze that it might have been me who was leaving while the others stayed put. I didn't have a clue. It must have been they who left, however, because I was still there. I drank some existential water and felt better.

– THE FRENCH AIR FORCE
CRACK SUICIDE SQUAD –

STEWART

I walked alone towards the centre of town on the croissant run the next morning. This was an optimistic mission, given that it was past ten o'clock and the chances of there being any remaining croissants or *pains au chocolat* at the *boulangeries* were minimal. Dull tourists in flip-flops waddled along in single file ahead of me, like a line of baby ducks in ridiculous shirts, and further on in the town square the usual groups of families were milling around, promising their bored kids they'd soon be leaving Castellane and heading for the south coast where interesting things happened.

The *boulangerie* in the square had a queue that extended out onto the pavement, so I took an alley to the backstreets where I knew of a relatively hidden shop that would attract far less custom. Once inside it I could see why. There was little more in this shop than a couple of tarts. One of them was about to serve me when an old peasant woman walked in and pushed in front of me, elbowing me aside with a thick arm. This appeared to be perfectly acceptable behaviour to the tart behind the counter, who chatted politely to the peasant while rudely ignoring me. I wasn't sure whether it was age, ignorance or arrogance that gave peasants the right to push in front of people, or maybe just being French sufficed, but I calmly accepted my social demotion to sub-peasant status and waited for the stodgy old prune to piss off.

Once more at the front of the queue (although only because I was the only one in it) I surveyed the options on the glass shelves around the room: a couple of burnt croissants; a small pile of dry bread; and some nasty, sticky pastries decorated with dead flies.

'*Deux croissants, une baguette, et une tarte aux mouches,*' I said, cheekily pointing to the things with flies on.

The woman seemed oddly unaffronted by my attitude, but I quickly realised that it was simply because she hadn't understood my French, despite an impeccable accent. An impeccable *English* accent, that is.

I repeated the order more slowly this time, and neglected to mention the flies.

'*Simon et Garfunkel*?' she asked as I paid her. She strummed an imaginary guitar and grinned inanely. All the locals called us *Simon et Garfunkel*, presumably with some irony since the American duo's harmonies were so tight it was as if their voices were on rails, while ours were on porridge. This was the eighth consecutive summer during which we had subjected them to our abbreviated, simplified and speeded-up renditions of *Bridge Over Troubled Water*, *The Boxer* and *Mrs Robinson*.

'*Ouai,*' I admitted, using my best colloquial, then rushed outside before she asked me to sing *Feelin' Groovy* for her.

Back in the square there were even more people than before, and most of them appeared to be looking in the same direction. I checked my flies. They were still on the cake. People's heads were all tilted towards the cliff that overlooked the town. It wasn't unusual to see tourists

42

craning their necks up to look at this rock and at the insane chapel located at its peak, but they were all looking slightly below the peak, at a clump of vegetation clinging precariously to the edge of the cliff, which was smouldering.

Cool, I thought.

A young Dutchwoman standing by me, who was fluent in more forms of communication than C3PO, explained that two days ago hundreds of fireworks had been set off from the bridge at the base of the rock to celebrate Bastille Day. Some of them had landed in the dry grass that grew on ledges high up on the cliff, and the hot sun yesterday had kept one of them smouldering all day. It had died down during the night, but was starting to flare up again this morning.

'Cool,' I said, noticing a tiny lick of flame dance up from the ledge.

The fire was at least a hundred feet above ground level, completely out of reach of any sane human. Even a Frenchman would have trouble getting there. But that didn't seem to matter. There were other grassy ledges, like scattered window boxes, all over the rough face of the cliff, but there wasn't any combustible material to connect them. The nearest dense vegetation was a Belgian walking up the path to the chapel, and just behind him, to the left of the rock, a dry wooded hillside curled around the back of the town. The gap between the embryonic fire and the hillside trees was at least fifty feet. There was no way this could escalate into anything especially interesting.

★

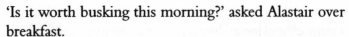

'Is it worth busking this morning?' asked Alastair over breakfast.

We had enough money to last us almost a day, so I didn't see any urgency in earning more.

'Not enough people around yet. No one's shopping or eating. They're all just looking at the fire on the mountain,' I told him, as if a boring volcano were erupting behind us.

'Cool,' said Paul, standing up in his boxer shorts to admire the spectacle. The fire on the ledge was burning steadily, sending sparks zig-zagging into the breeze.

I explained what had happened, as told to me by the Dutch babe I had met.

'That's amazing,' said Alastair. 'Was she blonde?'

We disposed of the remains of the repulsive breakfast close to a neighbour's tent, in order to draw ants away from our pitch, then commenced a stroll around the campsite to see if there were any girls staying there that we might like to sleep with.

'Five,' said Paul, upon completion of the tour.

'Seven,' said Alastair.

'Oh, I, er, lost count,' I said. 'Can you count mothers and daughters, or is it just one per family?'

'Not if they're Dutch,' said Paul.

'In that case, about twenty-two.'

It was twenty-two more than I was likely to be sleeping with, to be precise.

★

On the gravel at the front of the campsite some French peasants were playing *pétanque*. None smiled, and few words were spoken. Cigarettes burned slowly in their mouths until they grew short enough to be extinguished by the constant dribble on their lips. *Pétanque* was serious. They played it as if it actually mattered a sod whose ball was thrown closest to the jack. There was a *pétanque* competition on the campsite in a couple of days, bringing with it the opportunity of winning such glorious prizes as a bottle of wine from the local supermarket, or something equally shit, and these *surrendered-on-the-first-day-of-the-war* veterans were training up to eight hours a day in order to be The Best. They were France's Top Guns, an elite force of smelly, incoherent peasants with pin-point throwing abilities and extensions of nasal hair that should have required planning permission.

We steered a wide berth around them.

I challenged Paul to a game of ping-pong on the chipped concrete table next to the peasants. Once he had thrashed me it was Alastair's turn. Then we played table tennis. Losing at table tennis was something at which I excelled, but I chose not to make a career out of it.

In order to get over my defeat I took a stroll back into town on my own to see if there was any tacky souvenir crap I could buy from the cynical tourist shops. Rue du Mitan was chocablock with them: useless leather pieces of junk dyed blue and red with 'Castellane' printed on the front and 'China' printed on the back; pointless Castellane pottery made near Perpignan; and stripy bags with handles fitted with a self-destruct unit timed to snap the moment you get home at the end of the holiday. I was considering making such an unwise purchase when a saucy voice behind me said,

'*Salut. Ça va?*'

I knew that voice. It belonged to Castellane's hottest young vixen, Eva. She was in her dungarees, and part of the lizard tattooed on her breast was peeping at me.

'*Oui, ça va?*' I replied to the lizard. A puff of smoke enveloped me, through which I tried to see her face, but I had trouble seeing further than the end of her Marlboro *Heavy*. A breeze then cleared the smog, revealing her pretty face and *un-south-of-France-like* blonde hair and blue eyes. A very pleasant sight, I thought, just as the very pleasant sight vanished again behind an exhalation of gaseous tar.

'*Tu vas chanter?*' she asked, pretending to strum her cigarette like a guitar. This was a silly action: my guitar was nothing like as big as her fag. I told her yes, we were going to sing, possibly tonight. 'Cool,' she said. Clearly she hadn't heard us sing for some years.

'Do you want to come back to my place, bouncy-bouncy?' I asked, using a pointless Hungarian accent.

'*Comment?*' she replied, tilting her head like an inquisitive dog.

Perhaps I was too subtle for her. I had fancied Eva since we first visited this town seven years earlier, when she had been *totally* out of my league. She was the kind of girl who was given a double bed before she had even learnt to smoke in it. To her, sex was a basic daily necessity, like smoking drugs or shoplifting, and there was a plentiful supply of arrogant, greasy, hormonal, immature French males on mopeds to fulfil those needs. But I didn't care about the competition. The blokes who hung around her were dull, purposeless individuals whose only

46

hobby was combing the black fur on their chests and shoulders. They were *singes*; puny, primitive primordial creatures who would one day grow up to be slightly taller *singes* with pot bellies. She didn't seem to mind them, but that was because she didn't know any better. Now that I had stopped getting my hair cut at Blind Frank's Pudding Bowl Shop, I had more confidence. She now only seemed *slightly* out of my league. The trouble was finding a way to seduce her without lowering myself to the standards of my rivals for her affections. French types were used to more direct chat-up lines, such as, 'You will have sex with me tonight,' so no matter what I said to her she probably thought I was just trying to be sociable.

'*Tu veux sortir avec moi pour boire quelquechose?*' I asked her, instinctively miming a drinking action because I didn't expect her to understand me.

'*Quand?*'

'*Ce soir. Après la musique.*'

'*Oui,*' she said, with a slight whistle in her voice.

Blimey, I thought, that was easy. I should have asked for sex instead.

On the way back I bumped into Alastair and Paul sitting on a bench in the square. They were staring up at the burning cliff face. Smoke was now emanating from a couple of other ledges close to the original fire.

The fire was boring, I decided. It wasn't going to burn the town down.

★

All French people fall asleep at lunchtime. Thousands of years of natural selection have resulted in an automatic

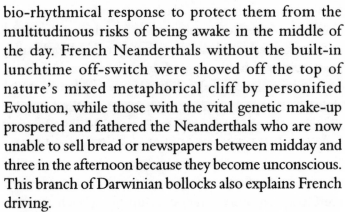
bio-rhythmical response to protect them from the multitudinous risks of being awake in the middle of the day. French Neanderthals without the built-in lunchtime off-switch were shoved off the top of nature's mixed metaphorical cliff by personified Evolution, while those with the vital genetic make-up prospered and fathered the Neanderthals who are now unable to sell bread or newspapers between midday and three in the afternoon because they become unconscious. This branch of Darwinian bollocks also explains French driving.

Thus it was that the town of Castellane fell briefly quiet this lunchtime, during a lull in which there wasn't even any Dutch or British holiday traffic passing through. But when, momentarily, Paul and Alastair stopped swearing at each other, their profanities were not replaced by silence. Instead, a gentle crackling sound filled the air around us, as if the mountain were munching a large packet of crisps. Smoky bacon flavour.

Up on the cliff face, about five or six ledges were now fully ablaze. One of these was sending sparks into the bracken at the edge of the hillside forest. The local *sapuer pompier* appeared to have the scene under control. He was on the hillside with his standard issue bucket of water, guiding the tourists down the slope and away from the path at the side of the burning cliff. He tipped a little from his bucket at a time onto each spark as it landed, but I suspected his system had a few inherent limitations. He realised this too once his bucket was empty and the sparks kept on coming. With everyone now safely off the hillside and Monsieur Moustache, the gendarme with a moustache for a face, blocking access to the footpath by attaching each end of his moustache to a fence post, the lone fireman trotted off to measure the length of his hose.

I was surprised and impressed to see the fireman return not only with a hose, but with some extra men, including old Monsieur Mistral, the owner of our campsite. I knew from our bizarre conversations that he had been a fireman in Napoleonic times, and it was heartening to see him rejuvenated by the thrill of fighting fires again armed with nothing more than a hosepipe and a cigarette. Normally all we would get by way of conversation from Monsieur Mistral were French renditions of 'Long live the Queen' and 'Beware of Belgian girls', no matter what we said to him, so any remotely sane dialogue usually came as a shock. I once stayed on his campsite having driven there in an old Volvo estate, and found him sitting in it one morning, playing with the wheel, and talking about how it was more solidly built than the tank he drove in the war.

Several long hoses now snaked up the hill close to the fire. The original fires on the cliff ledges had now burned themselves out, leaving only smoking embers, but their offspring on the hillside were proliferating wildly. The clear blue sky over Castellane was stained by a black cloud that hung stubbornly overhead, and its size was widening as the fire spread further across the hillside. An uninhabited, medieval tower, part of the old town walls used as a look-out for invasions of German tourists, was the first building in the path of the fire. A few yards further across the hill were the houses at the back of the town. I could hear the shouts of the firemen becoming desperate.

'This is going to be cool,' said Paul.

One of the firemen started running down the hill, away from the fire, leaving his hose untended. I assumed he had run out of cigarettes and was popping over to the tobacconist's for some more, but I was wrong: he had a whole packet on him, and stopped next to a public telephone booth to light one up. He then made a quick call, took another deep drag, and ran back up to the fire.

The battle was evidently being lost. A true forest fire was now raging, beating back the feeble efforts of the *sapeurs pompiers*, and drawing large crowds of tourists with camcorders and cameras. Local people were mucking in to help the firemen, but we could see that the fire was spreading rapidly up and across the hill, mostly out of their reach. If it continued at that rate it could destroy Castellane within hours, demolishing defensive walls that had stood for a thousand years, burning everyone's pizzas and ruining my plans to date Eva that evening.

There were shouts on the hillside, and a rapid retreat took place. All the firemen and their assistants ran down towards the town, dragging their hoses behind them. This seemed oddly defeatist, even given their war record, but their reasons soon became apparent. From behind us came a small squadron of military aircraft, about seven in number, flying perilously low over the mountains that ringed the town. On approach to Castellane they formed an orderly line and dipped even lower, the noise of their engines screaming into our ears as they hurtled just above our heads towards the blazing hillside.

'Hurrah for the French Air Force Crack Suicide Squad,' said Paul as the first plane dived towards the fire.

There was a gasp from the astonished crowd in the town square. None of them had realised the French Air Force possessed this many planes. Each pilot in turn took his plane down to thirty or forty feet, released a ton of water from some kind of bomb bay onto the fire, then pulled back hard in order to follow the upward slope of the hill. This required a change in pitch of at least forty-five degrees and it had to be executed with split-second precision to avoid adding aviation fuel and assorted wreckage to the blaze. Towards the top of the hill they then had to veer sharply to the right in order to squeeze through a tight gap in the rocks.

With all the aircraft safely through, a small portion of the burning hill had been converted to steaming cinders. The planes flew off in the direction of the lake, and in their place came a helicopter which dropped a load of red chilli powder onto the flames. What the forest fire needed now was some tomato purée and garlic, but all it got was more water when the aircraft returned. They repeated their original crazy manoeuvres, dampening another part of the fire.

It was a truly impressive spectacle, requiring as much skill from the pilots as it takes to circumnavigate safely the Paris *péripherique*. We speculated that they were refilling from the lake between each attack. How this was achieved without landing, crashing or stopping for a cigarette we weren't sure, but they took less than ten minutes to reload each time. From our vantage point it didn't seem possible that so many of these attack runs could be undertaken without an accident. Their job seemed more hazardous than the Dambusters raids, and many of those plucky chaps in Lancasters bought it.

Throughout the afternoon the free show continued until the fire was out and Castellane was saved. The planes dropped their final loads, roared upwards into the sky, then turned back to their base, passing once more over the town. The last one cockily dipped his wings back and forth as he flew over, resulting in cheers and waves from a grateful crowd.

'Bastard show-off,' observed Paul. 'I wouldn't trust him to fly a kite.'

'A wise precaution,' I said.

★

We started work at 7.30 that evening, scrounging free glasses of wine from Philipe's crêperie and de-tuning our guitars for twenty minutes before plucking up the courage to begin. Singing in public gave us quite a buzz once we were into the swing of it, especially if the police used electric stun-guns to shut us up, but we were always apathetic about it and the first song would usually be delayed for as long as we could come up with excuses. Tonight, however, I felt different. While the others debated asking for a top-up in their wine glasses prior to commencing the gig, I was desperate to get it all over with so that I could meet Eva. I speeded up the songs as fast as I dared that night: *Yesterday* almost broke the sound barrier. Finally, when the set was finished, I left Paul and Alastair to collect the money. I didn't care about my share of the proceeds.

Eva was where she said she would be, seated at Bar le Glacier. I thought she looked ravishing, but unfortunately so did the twelve or so escaped monkeys seated around her. Did she really expect me to take part in this chimps' tea party? She stood up and kissed me on both cheeks, at which point I expected to hear the swish of a flick-knife rushing towards me from one of her simians, but they were too busy picking fleas off each other and talking about their mopeds. I recognised a couple of her semi-evolved friends from previous trips to Castellane, and we exchanged aggressive glares.

The only available chair was next to these unsavoury chaps, and there were still two more gorillas between myself and Eva. This wasn't good enough. It was pointless trying to fit in with their grunted conversations. The French I had been taught at school consisted of arty, elegant, and fundamentally useless bollocks like Molière and Balzac, rather than the real French that people actually spoke. I had endured many hours being taught how to use the subjunctive tense, which is not even used by French people, but not for one second was I taught how to chat-up a raunchy French girl or how to order a pizza without anchovies. Feeling mightily pissed-off with the anti-climax of it all, I walked away and called Eva over to me.

'*Je voudrais parler avec toi, pas avec le cast de Planet of the Apes*,' I told her.

'*Ils sont que bébés, putain. Ils m'emmerdent*,' she replied.

This was certainly not part of the Oxford Examining Board syllabus, but I guessed that *emmerder* was a verb that seemed to mean 'to piss off', or more literally, 'to

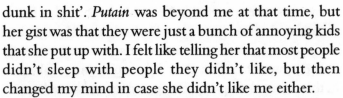

dunk in shit'. *Putain* was beyond me at that time, but her gist was that they were just a bunch of annoying kids that she put up with. I felt like telling her that most people didn't sleep with people they didn't like, but then changed my mind in case she didn't like me either.

Godzilla shouted something at Eva, and I guessed she wanted to go back and sit down.

'*Est-ce que tu veux voir le grand spectacle demain avec moi? Jusque toi et moi,*' I said. The *grand spectacle* to which I referred was anything but. It consisted of Monsieur Synth, a cheap clone of John Michael Jar or whatever his name was, and a bank of over-amplified synthesisers on which he would play out of date music from beneath an even older haircut. It was a thoroughly appalling form of entertainment, but one over which French types got embarrassingly orgasmic. I knew from previous visits of this pathetic musician that the decibels produced by his machines would make busking in any part of the town impossible, so I was free for a date at any time.

We agreed to try again tomorrow.

– Hot Goat And Chunks Of Lard –

PAUL

With Stewart's imminent date fast approaching, it occurred to Alastair and me that tonight was not going to follow the predictable course of previous evenings. That is, there would only be two of us.

'Are we busking tonight then, Ginge?' I asked Alastair. I needn't have bothered really: I knew the answer. I had all the musical ability of a hippo and the dexterity and swift actions of a tree sloth, something of which Alastair used to insist on reminding me on frequent occasions. The others didn't need my input on their busking missions, indeed I may even have hindered their efforts. They were humouring me by letting me play with them. But you knew that anyway – I am a bass player. Alastair decided to try tact on this occasion, however.

'Not sure, mate. Town looks a bit quiet tonight.'

That was all I needed really. I didn't fancy the thought of busking with him only. As I mentioned, the other two together were a tight, cohesive outfit that delivered note perfect renditions of songs our parents would have grooved to, while crooning along in harmony with each other. When I was accompanying them we had the same thing with a muffled bass-line and a rare, wobbly backing vocal. Each of us in isolation however was not quite tenable as a musical entity in our own right. I am a talentless, tone-deaf bassist (if you'll pardon the tautology), Stewart possesses a strumming style that is so wooden you could make furniture out of it and Alastair, although saddled with perfect pitch and a slightly

55

more rock 'n' roll voice, can't remember lyrics or refrain from creating his own time signatures. The mental picture of Alastair singing one half of the harmony from one song while ignoring my shaky succession of semiquavers from another was not appealing. 'We're on strike tonight, Stewart,' he declared once Stewart had returned from the bogs.

'Fine. Whatever,' was the reply. Stewart was thinking with his nob now so anything we said would have elicited a similar response.

I rolled a joint out of the remains of the *herbes de Provence* while Alastair contemplated the ignominy of spending an entire evening with a bass player. We stayed around the tent, drinking and smoking long after Stewart had departed on his daring and probably unsanitary mission. The conversation as ever started on women, progressed onto cars, houses and how unlikely it was that we'd ever be able to afford any of them. When the discussion reached subcutaneous soft-tissue medicine we decided it might be time to eat something.

★

Elien was as perennial a sight in Castellane as we were. Every summer the Algerian waitress would migrate to the town to work in a bar on the corner of the square serving Belgian beer to Dutch tourists who would be speaking English to Swedes. Or something. Although paid a pittance to work around eighteen hours a day, she seemed happy with her lot – her lot being chain-smoking floppy, African cigarettes with one hand while balancing an impossibly large and lopsided tray on the other.

'*Bonsoir*,' she gushed, momentarily removing the camel dung cigarette from her mouth while she gave us a couple of kisses each. '*Pas de musique?*' she enquired while miming the obligatory but stupid-looking strumming action with her cigarette arm. We explained that in a brief moment of clemency, the town of Castellane had been spared a further evening of sonic torture but that the reprieve would be unlikely to last longer than next morning.

'*Dommage*,' she replied, though whether she thought it was a shame that we weren't playing or a shame that our silence was only to last for one night was not clear. I suspect the former, given the insane loyalty shown to us by waiters who heard the same rubbish night after night, and yet still encouraged and gave us money even though we were decimating their tips.

We sat at a table as far from the restaurant as possible so that we would be as near as possible to the passing throng of female tourists. This was a pathetic reason as we both knew but we were pretty desperate and anything was worth a try. The menu provided a source of great amusement with its hilarious multi-lingual translations of the local specialities. I can't speak for the Dutch, Spanish or Italians but if you were English or German-speaking the menu contained a wealth of culinary descriptions which appeared to have been lifted, word-for-word, from a dictionary.

'Light broth of sea fruits?' suggested Alastair.

'Nah. I've got my eye on "herbal pig meat of the hills" with a side order of "various garden leafs when in season".'

In the end we settled on a couple of 'mountain shepherd pizzas with hot goat and chunks of lard' which was remarkably tastier than its title suggested.

STEWART

My second attempt at dating Eva started off well. We met in the main square, close to where Monsieur Synth was playing fifties rock 'n' roll tunes with eighties synthesiser sounds. It was like being taken back in time to the dark days when people thought that Mini Moogs sounded better than real musical instruments and leg warmers were at the cutting edge of fashion. Eva was on her own, smoking a cigarette from one of the many packs she always carried with her like a life-support system.

We spent a pleasant couple of minutes together, trying to ignore the offensive electronic sounds, talking in French about her life story. It was hard concentrating on getting the stupid language right when I was gazing into such beautiful blue eyes, even if they were always looking in directions other than mine. She seemed edgy about something, as if her headmaster was on the prowl and might catch her smoking at any minute.

'Je dois partir. C'est les bébés. Desolé, Stewart.'

'A demain?'

'Oui, bien sur.'

Across the square I could see the two 'babies' who had glared at me the night before, and who now seemed to have forced Eva's early departure from my company. She rushed over to them, hoping they hadn't noticed that she had been with me. This was getting frustrating, like trying to get an intimate moment with a cashpoint machine when there were always people queuing behind you to press her magic buttons. Oh well, until tomorrow, I thought to myself.

– VOULEZ-VOUS PÉTANQUER AVEC MOI (CE SOIR)? –

PAUL

I have noticed how the French can become really excited at the most trivial, dated and dull things. Such was the case in Monsieur Mistral's *pétanque* tournament. The opportunity to become part of sporting history was open to all who chose to stay at this prestigious site. Though none of us had ever played before, we were all well aware that when it came to *pétanque* – a serious matter to any Frenchman – the French were a bunch of cheating bastards. This had become apparent on the many times we had watched the local peasants doing their thing in the town square: a spectacle that inexplicably attracted huge audiences. As Gaston walked over to his ball to ascertain if he had thrown the closest, Marcel from the other team would distract him by dropping a coin or cigarette while Hugo, his team-mate, would unsubtly flick any winning balls from the opposing team away from the jack with his foot. The crowd would remain silent during this as if nothing had happened – a stark contrast to the only sport I ever watch in England, where the slightest infraction of the rules invokes a ten-thousand voice strong shout of 'Handball!' or 'Oi! You dirty northern bastards!' Still, sound in this knowledge, we were at least prepared, though we doubted our Britishness would allow us to sink to their level when it came to cheating.

Registration was at ten o'clock at the camp office. The arrival of this time brought a small crowd of French campers, each trying to push in front of the other in order to be first on the list. We couldn't be bothered to involve ourselves in the melée so Alastair and I had a smoke while Stewart chose to take a shit around the corner. After the hubbub had ended we simply approached Monsieur Mistral and indicated that we would like to participate too. Monsieur Mistral eyed us in a suspicious manner.

'Vous? Vous voulez jouer?' he asked barely able to believe us.

'Bien sûr. Pourquoi pas?'

'Car vous êtes "Rosbif". Anglais.'

He wasn't wrong: we were indeed roast beef, English, but we were unperturbed by this in much the same way as the members of the Jamaican bobsleigh team were, when they registered for the Winter Olympics in Calgary. So what if we were English? Normally the English invent games, teach foreigners how to play them and then spend the rest of eternity wishing they hadn't. Why not try some reverse logic? Monsieur Mistral was probably correct. There was every chance that we would be soundly thrashed in a game of which we had no experience, but we didn't care and we stood resolute in our decision to play. He rolled his eyes in wonder at us then, pointing his stubby, chewed pencil at Stewart, his face took on a puzzled look. He looked at me for a few seconds then back at Stewart.

'Ton frère?' He pointed the masticated pencil at me. Stewart and I had often pretended that we were brothers; not for any particular reason, just that we liked to see just how much bullshit we could get away with.

'*Oui, mon frère,*' affirmed Stewart hesitantly.

Monsieur Mistral then performed some gesticulations which we took to be asking who was the eldest. On this occasion I assumed the mantle of 'Old Knacker'.

'*Ah bon. Famille, c'est bon. Enregistrez ici.*'

As we had committed ourselves to the untruth of being related, I now found myself having to write my name wrongly. We'd checked in using Stewart's passport so on this occasion I would have to be a Ferris. In turn we each wrote our names. What we forgot, of course, is that we hadn't written them as we should have – I had remembered to assume the name of Paul Ferris, but this wasn't enough, it would transpire.

At midday, the hottest, and therefore most appropriate, time of day to be bent double under the sun, a swarm of eager campers gathered under the large horse-chestnut tree in front of the camp office. To us *Rosbif*, the excitement seemed more than was warranted for such a trivial occasion but the French were in high spirits, babbling among themselves and bragging about who would acquire the mighty accolade of Camp Pétanque Champion. Monsieur Mistral cleared his throat and theatrically held up his opening speech in front of him. He then revealed to the expectant horde that not only would there be a possibility of winning a bottle of wine worth up to nine Francs but also that the winning team would receive a signed certificate to remember the tournament by. We were completely overawed by the majesty of the occasion. While on the subject of teams, Monsieur Mistral thought it only fair to warn the rest of the competitors that three of them would have their chances of victory seriously impeded by being paired with an Englishman. There was a hushed gasp from the assembled *pétanquers*.

'*Les Chanteurs Anglais*,' he proclaimed to a reception of total indifference. Monsieur Mistral began to pull names from a hat so disgustingly brown that even he wouldn't wear it. We chatted amongst ourselves while this was happening – Alastair was secretly hoping to be 'coupled' with a nubile Dutch girl he had noticed. Though he had never spoken to her he had decided that not only did she fancy him but also that she took it up the *achterste*. This was a pointless but fascinating conversation but nevertheless had engrossed us to the point that we did not notice Monsieur Mistral calling us.

'*Ferreeee Stewaaaarrr*,' he cried. He must be calling a Belgian we decided. Monsieur Mistral knew who he meant, though. After shouting this strange utterance several times he walked right up to us, pointed first at Stewart, then at Stewart's name on the piece of paper he was holding and repeated himself.

'Think that's you, mate.' Stewart sauntered off to join his unsuspecting team-mate. It dawned on us that old Monsieur Mistral had got our names arse-about-face because we'd neither written our surnames first nor in capital letters. This had completely bamboozled Mistral of course and, recognising neither the word 'Stewart' nor 'Ferris' he was none the wiser. This was an understandable mistake we decided. The situation did become stranger, though, as he hailed me as '*Ferreeee Pol*'.

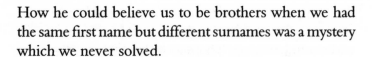

How he could believe us to be brothers when we had the same first name but different surnames was a mystery which we never solved.

★

The 'lucky' person to acquire the Bassett handicap that afternoon was a French girl called Stephanie. She did not try to hide her disappointment from me and started complaining about how unfair life was to her dad, until I let her know that I could understand exactly what she was saying.

As it turned out, my Anglo-French team didn't fare too badly. Stephanie didn't particularly care for my cavalier attitude towards what was, for her, a matter of pride. I think we made it to the quarter-finals but were knocked out by a couple of foul-smelling peasants dressed in onion sacks.

The cheating, though, was there as expected. This time it took a different form from that to which I was accustomed. One peasant tried to lull me into a false sense of security by insisting that we measure the distance between the jack and each of our pétanque balls with a stalk of dry grass. First he would hold one end of the grass to the jack and then pinch the stalk between his thumb and forefinger. Then he would look up to me all doe-eyed as if to say 'see, that's how far my ball is away'. As he stood up he would let the stem slip between his fingers so that he had magically gained another inch to his advantage. If this mode of cheating was still not going to be enough to secure victory, the peasant would accidentally knock our ball away from the jack with the back of his hand as he knelt down to measure. Sometimes he would flatly deny that he had touched it, other times he would generously move our ball back towards the jack about half as much as he had knocked it away in the first place.

I didn't care that we hadn't won; the fact that we hadn't been thrashed and that we'd actually beaten some of the most fancied competitors was reward enough. I was lucky enough, however, to win a bottle of *vin de pays de l'Hérault* for my trouble. It smelled like a badger's arse so we drowned some insects in it and then poured it down the drain.

STEWART

The excitement and drama of the crappy *pétanque* competition was almost sufficient to distract me from wondering whether tonight's date with Eva would be more successful than the previous ones. Usually she would walk past us during our busking sessions, but tonight she was nowhere to be seen among the throngs of tourists in the narrow Castellane streets. None of the *singes* was there, either. Very odd, I thought.

After 'work', we settled down outside Jo-Jo's to mellow out and drink. Strangely, though, the place was devoid of both Eva and the monkeys. Without the billowing smoke and the high-pitched chatter of the simians, the place seemed to have no atmosphere. I went inside to see if she might be hiding in some discreet recess, but there were only two old men seated around the bar. One of them I recognised as Louis, who had been mayor of Castellane about fifty years ago, and who was now in his nineties. He wore piss-stained trousers with the flies

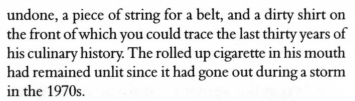

undone, a piece of string for a belt, and a dirty shirt on the front of which you could trace the last thirty years of his culinary history. The rolled up cigarette in his mouth had remained unlit since it had gone out during a storm in the 1970s.

I didn't recognise the other old man, and was therefore horrified when he stood up and introduced himself to me. He explained that he was the father of *Monsieur Rafting* (his real name is being protected because I can't remember it), a friendly enough sort who wore barmy trousers, owned the local whitewater rafting business and always said hello to us when we were busking. I acknowledged that this was wonderful news and looked around desperately for Eva.

'I speak a little English,' said Monsieur Rafting Senior.

'Oh shit,' I thought. 'Here we go.'

He came a little closer and spoke some more.

'I came to England and fought with the English during the war. I had to learn your language so that I could make love to your women.'

Suddenly he ceased, despite his proximity to Louis, to be a peasant. He spoke English, which was rare enough in France, and he was a war hero, which was unheard of in those collaborative parts.

'I went to North Africa under Field Marshall Montgomery,' he told me, swallowing the last of his beer.

'*Vraiment? Donc vous étiez là avec mon grandpère. Ça c'est incroyable!*' I said, lapsing into French at the shock of meeting someone who had actually fought alongside my grandfather in the war. I bought him a beer, and hoped that Louis would stay silent during our discourse because

66

I knew I wouldn't be able to communicate with him if he tried to talk in his extreme patois.

'We used to put the legs of our camp beds in buckets of diesel to stop the bugs climbing onto us during the night,' said Monsieur Rafting Senior as I passed him a fresh beer. 'There was no beer in the desert,' he added. 'When we ran out of water we had to drink from the radiator in our truck.'

Somehow, even the worst aspects of Inter-Railing seemed pleasant when I thought about that: Paul's feet; sleeping in toilets; even Belgium seemed palatable compared to having to fight Jerry on a bellyful of anti-freeze and sand. I felt connected to this man by history. It had taken fifty years for his path to cross with the grandson of one of his fellow soldiers, and I felt a profound sense of unworthiness in his presence. He had drunk anti-freeze for my freedom, and all I could repay him with was a beer. Life's weird like that, sometimes. He didn't seem to mind.

Having agreed with the Desert Rat that the size of the world tended towards the diminutive, I said goodbye and went back outside to the others.

'No sign of the old trout, then?' asked Paul.

I gave up on seeing Eva that night, and just relaxed with my drink. Every now and then a delicate splash from the fountain would land on my face, and the only sounds were the gentle murmurs of Paul's underwear.

'Boom-boom-cha-cha,' came a thunderous sound that snapped me out of my mellowness.

'What the fuck is that meant to be?' asked Alastair.

The space in the corner of the little square was now

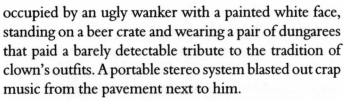

occupied by an ugly wanker with a painted white face, standing on a beer crate and wearing a pair of dungarees that paid a barely detectable tribute to the tradition of clown's outfits. A portable stereo system blasted out crap music from the pavement next to him.

'It's Marcel-bloody-Marceau,' I said.

The mime's eyes looked nervously around him while his arms attempted to move in the fashion of a fake robot that was being played by a bad actor. The waiter arrived with the bill, and I asked him why such an affront to dignity and decency was being permitted to perform before my very eyes.

'*Q'est-ce que c'est, ce merde?*' I asked.

'*C'est l'Automat,*' he replied, with worrying enthusiasm. '*C'est cool, non?*'

'*Non,*' I confirmed.

The Automat had shifted his centre of gravity too far to one side, and fell awkwardly off his perch. Had he a spark of charisma within him, he might have been able to laugh off the incident by incorporating it into his 'act', if you could call it that, but instead he decided to rewind the cassette and start again. Synonyms for pain cannot begin to describe our suffering.

I looked around the square at the French people who were emerging from doorways and alleys to watch the non-spectacle. When the Automat managed to get through a whole routine without falling off his beer crate they cheered and clapped as if they had actually been entertained by something. It was all extremely bemusing.

'If he doesn't fuck off back to the circus I'm going to throw him in the fountain,' offered Paul.

'Maybe the point is that he's mimicking a shite mime artist,' said Alastair.

'It's pretty bloody convincing,' I added. 'Come on. Let's just get Monsieur Moustache to arrest him.'

Alas, Castellane's moustachioed crime fighter was nowhere to be seen. We left Jo-Jo's and its demented mime person thing and retired to the peace and sanity of our campsite where the mad owner and his slightly less mad wife could be heard having a shouting match in their kitchen.

– THE RETURN OF MONSIEUR SILENCE –

STEWART

Alastair spent the day pontificating about the bloody Automat and the effect he would have on our profits if he chose to stick around. I spent the day thinking about Eva. This was a bad sign; it meant my unrequited lust for her was affecting me too much, preventing me from relaxing and ogling other women instead.

To confirm our worst fears, the Automat arrived at the pizzeria while we were tucking into our free pizzas. Unbelievably, he was warmly greeted by the restaurant owners and shown the best place to begin his appalling act, which was just a few feet from our table. I suddenly felt physically sick, and the luscious, slimy pizza lost its appeal. The Automat went through the same dull, amateurish moves as the night before, lasting a full half hour. Why didn't he rehearse in private, like most entertainers? I wondered. Why was he even born?

I put some worthless Centimes into his hat when he had finished. Paul contributed some of his pizza. The Automat poured the contents of his hat into his pocket without examining them, and quickly disappeared. Two minutes later we could hear his repulsive music booming along the alley from the square at Jo-Jo's. Already two of our busking venues had been milked. It was time to rush around to a virgin site before he extracted all the loose change in the town.

Eva came over to me just as we were about to start busking outside the ironically named Auberge de bon Accueil, the miserable proprietor of which had

70

reluctantly granted permission for our singing. Eva's head was bowed as if almost being sorry for having stood me up the night before. By way of revenge, I refused to speak to her or even acknowledge her for a full ten seconds.

It turned out that a bunch of monkeys on mopeds had virtually kidnapped her yesterday afternoon and rode up to the lake so that they could all take their clothes off and swing from the trees into the water. Eva had been the only girl in the group, quite possibly the only Homo sapiens too, but she had been 'bored' by them all, probably in more ways than one.

The busking finished early that night, to my immense relief. There was no point trying to exploit pitches already polluted by the Automat, so we accepted a reduced income with bad grace. I rushed off to meet Eva at Jo-Jo's, then we went to a less popular bar that would give us more privacy.

She had barely smoked her first packet of cigarettes when I asked her a question that had been bothering me for some time: where did she get her blonde hair? She told me she had been born in Marseille where this was a rarity, but her family roots were far more exotic. Her great grandmother, it seemed, was a member of the Russian royal family who had fled to Poland during the revolution. There she had married a Pole, and the couple then moved to the south of France where they led a comfortable life as wealthy aristocrats. Eva told me about her memories of her grandfather's house and servants, and the chauffeured Rolls Royce in which he travelled during the seventies. Her family now was completely broke, living in a small apartment next to a railway line

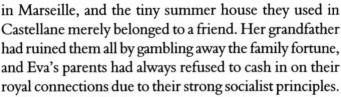

in Marseille, and the tiny summer house they used in Castellane merely belonged to a friend. Her grandfather had ruined them all by gambling away the family fortune, and Eva's parents had always refused to cash in on their royal connections due to their strong socialist principles.

So, young Eva had turned out to be a penniless Russian princess. And I thought she was just another Frog. I wasn't used to dating princesses, but I figured the best approach would be to tempt her back to my tent, and to hope that Paul had put his dirty washing away.

'Would you like to come back to the tent for some chocolate and a shag?' I asked her.

'*Quoi? Non!*' she replied.

'What's the matter? Don't you like chocolate?'

Not all girls love chocolate, of course, and I wasn't the sort to force it on them. But I was quite happy to eat chocolate on my own, if necessary, so I took her hand on a no-obligation basis and led her back to the campsite. We sat outside my tent, talking rubbish, stroking each other's hands and resisting the bar of chocolate next to us.

Finally, I told her I'd like a snog. She moved closer and we kissed for a full five, magical seconds. Then she stood up and said she had to go, and took off for town at a running pace.

Dejected after the anti-climax of my five second romance with Eva, I wandered back into town to find the chaps. I discovered them seated near the fountain at Jo-Jo's talking to a disgustingly healthy-looking French bloke and a female who looked like Wonderwoman, only blonde.

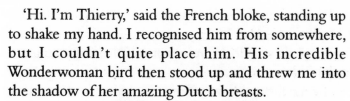

'Hi. I'm Thierry,' said the French bloke, standing up to shake my hand. I recognised him from somewhere, but I couldn't quite place him. His incredible Wonderwoman bird then stood up and threw me into the shadow of her amazing Dutch breasts.

'My name is Wonderwoman,' said Wonderwoman. Her name was actually a beautiful Dutch name, which I can't spell, and which probably translates as Wonderwoman anyway. Her olive-oiled skin glistened under the street light and her teeth shone like the crescent moon.

I could feel my knees wobble.

'Wow,' I said, proffering my hand and looking straight at her solid bosoms, which were at my eye level.

Paul explained to me that Thierry had been *Monsieur Silence* in our previous book, *Don't Lean Out of the Window!*, but that he was no longer our enemy having left the employment of Camp du Verdon and the despotic *Monsieur Fash*.

'So you were working there when we burnt those picnic tables at the camp fire five years ago?' I asked.

'That was you? I don't believe it!' Thierry exclaimed. 'I nearly lost my job because of that night. You have no idea of the trouble you caused by burning those tables.'

Thierry was getting quite excited about this.

'My boss refused to replace those tables after you burnt them. There will never be picnic tables on the campsite again.' He was gesticulating now, endangering the existence of the glasses on our table.

'Cool,' said Paul.

'I'm sorry,' said Thierry, 'you are right. I must stay cool. It doesn't matter now.'

'You're not a fascist anymore, Thierry,' said Paul. 'Mellow out, man.'

'What do you do, Wonderwoman?' I asked, trying not to dribble.

'I save little children from drowning in swimming pools,' she replied, modestly.

'Actually,' added Thierry, 'she's also in the Dutch Olympic swimming team. She won a silver in the last games.'

I wiped the saliva from my chin as I imagined her in a swimsuit, her short blonde hair clinging wet against her head, her cold nipples bursting through the fabric, and her moist lips poised to breathe the kiss of life into some lucky bastard.

'Are you alright?' Alastair asked me.

'Jugs,' I croaked.

'Precisely,' he agreed.

'What do you do in Holland?' asked Paul to Thierry.

'I am a swimming instructor. I teach Dutch girls to swim, and they teach me things, too.'

'I bet they do,' I said.

'I have learned to speak Dutch very well by being in the water with young girls.'

'Beats Linguaphone,' I observed.

'How did you learn English, though?' asked Paul.

'From listening to records and singing the songs. I learned English by reading the lyrics to Led Zeppelin songs. I play guitar as well, you know,' he said, looking at Paul.

'As well as who?' asked Paul, looking to see if there were any musicians in the vicinity.

'As well as you guys,' said the former fascist and current shagger of Wonderwoman.

'You're too kind,' said Paul.

Wonderwoman stood up and stretched her goddess-like body.

'Come on darling,' she said, taking Thierry's hand, 'I want sex.'

With that, poor Thierry was dragged off and forced to do unimaginable things to her all night long. But I tried imagining them, anyway.

– CLONK, CLONK, BAAA! –

PAUL

'Clonk, clonk, baaa! Clonk, clonk, baaa!'

I woke up more irritably than usual. So did the others. It was four-thirty in the morning. This surprised us all: though we had heard of there being a four-thirty in the morning as well as the afternoon, none of us had ever experienced it.

'Clonk, clonk, baaa!'

'Are you shagging a Welsh bird in your smeggy sleeping bag?' enquired Alastair.

'Who? Me or Stewart?'

'Stewart of course. No one would shag you: not even a Welsh chick.'

In fact, none of us was involved in any kind of ovine sex. We had been woken up by Castellane's rush hour. Through a gap in the tent doors came not only the freezing cold down-draught of dawn air but also the surreal sight of an endless stream of sheep. The procession filled the entire width of the road and stretched as far as we could see in either direction. Some families had got up and out of their centrally heated, satellite television equipped caravans to admire the spectacle but we stayed put, deeply unimpressed.

We tried going back to sleep but it was no good. I wriggled out of the tent and stood in the dew-soaked grass in my boxer shorts while I smoked a cigarette. I liked to think I looked like Robert Duvall in *Apocalypse Now* but the truth was certainly far less glamorous.

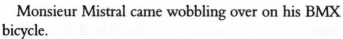

Monsieur Mistral came wobbling over on his BMX bicycle.

'*Des moutons!*' he observed as if I had never seen sheep before.

'*Oui, je sais,*' I replied irritably.

'*Il y a des moutons en Angleterre?*' he asked.

I explained that we did indeed have sheep in England but the reason he was unaware of their existence was that most of them seemed to end up consumed by fire at some French roadblock or other in Normandy before they had a chance to get any further inland. He uttered something I didn't understand but probably meant either 'What a wag you are with your quick and ready wit!' or 'You British smartarse! Why don't you just fuck off?' He disappeared on his bike while I pondered which of these pseudo-translations I was going to believe.

'Go and the get the croissants, Fatty,' ordered the disembodied voice of Alastair from deep within the bowels of the tent. Bowels of the tent is a particularly fitting metaphor for reasons which probably do not require any explanation. With that, a pair of Converse All-Stars and a T-shirt flew though the tent doors and landed in the wet grass.

'Yeah, and I'll have three *pains au chocolat*,' added Stewart. 'Get yourself something nice too,' he added as a salvo of loose change came flying out of the tent and distributed itself over a wide area of dewy grass. Without giving the matter too much thought, I slipped my wet feet into my damp boots and pulled the T-shirt on over my head. It was inside out but that didn't matter. That's one of the things I love about being on holiday abroad – there is no way at home that I would walk into a town centre at dawn wearing a pair of unlaced boots and my underwear, but here, away from anyone who might give a damn, it was not even the slightest worry.

Arriving in town, however, I realised the inherent flaw in the plan. Nothing was open. There was only an unhealthy amount of activity as the town got ready for the day's business. 'What's wrong with nine to five-thirty?' I wondered. I tried the bakery door but it was indeed locked. One of the tarts inside shooed me away with a contemptuous look. What was the matter with her? I was only a semi-naked English tourist wanting food at five in the morning. What could be more normal than that?

I wondered whether my carbohydrate-gathering mission would turn out to be a waste of effort – the others would probably have drifted off back to sleep by the time I got back leaving me on my own to devour any breakfast I managed to procure. Eventually, having given up, I noticed a man carrying a plastic crate full of bread from the open door of a building to a waiting van. With some linguistic difficulty I managed to persuade the baker in his little bread factory to part with a quantity of greasy, French breakfast materials. He looked confused by the whole incident but I had got what I had come for.

Back at the tent my suspicions were confirmed as I found the others asleep in the tent. I ate my breakfast and forced my way back into what had been my sleeping area before I had so foolishly vacated it. I left the rest of the croissants outside for the ants to eat . . . or at least to defecate on.

With nothing on the agenda for today we decided to laze around the tent picking holes in everyone and everything that was unfortunate enough to stray into our line of sight. The first victims were members of a group of hikers. Their support vehicle arrived in mid-morning to set up their tents for them. This struck us as being a bit poncey. Why didn't these people carry their own tents around on their backs? That is not to say that we wouldn't jump at the chance of having someone carrying all our crap around for us while we gallivanted about France annoying people and getting drunk. The tents were identical blue affairs much like ours but probably lacking the accompanying odours and stains. Their perfectly formed ridges formed a faultless line along the side of the site nearest the town. We hypothesised over who might be coming to sleep in them later. Naturally, our first hope was a group of eighteen year old Dutch girls on a sex crusade across the south of France, then we thought that maybe the tents would be occupied by Girl Guides. The others were quite excited by the prospect but I could not think of a Girl Guide without thinking of one or other of my sisters in that uniform. This obviously did not make for good sexual imaginings, though it may have done if I had been brought up in the Fens of East Anglia.

When the occupants of the perfect blue tents did finally arrive in late afternoon we were disappointed, but by no means surprised, to discover that the party seemed to comprise single men and women in the thirty to sixty age range. They were attired in the brightest Lycra and the most modern and expensive Gore-Tex. They looked like they actually enjoyed walking as a means of travelling from A to B. We could not get our minds around that philosophy. I watched as they washed their socks, read novels and wrote postcards outside their tents: this was like being camped next to our parents which, in itself, was too much. We decided that though it was a little early in the evening, the best way to avoid these spectres of dullness would be to escape to town where we could drink beer and ogle women while waiting for fresh tourists with money to burn and no appreciation of music. In a word: Belgians.

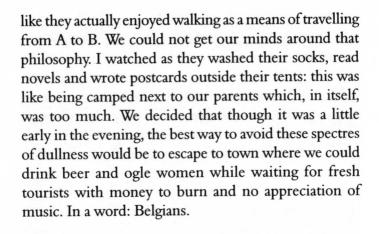

– MONSIEUR RAFTING AND MONSIEUR HAIR BEAR –

STEWART

Monsieur Rafting had been urging us for some time to sacrifice ourselves on one of his rafting expeditions. These involved hurtling downstream in a patched-up piece of inflated rubber, bouncing over the many protrusions from the river bed – large boulders, sharp rocks and the remains of previous expeditions. The chances of surviving the treacherous Gorges du Verdon in this manner were similar to those of a mouse caught in a kitchen sink waste disposal unit, so it was hugely popular with the sensible local French types.

There seemed to be a healthy covering of water over the razor blades and broken glass in the Verdon this morning, so we took a stroll over to Monsieur Rafting's house to see if there was a leaky dinghy into which we could squeeze. He lived about a couple of miles out of Castellane, past Camp du Verdon and a bit further along the Gorge, which was for us quite an expedition in itself. We followed the 'rafting' signs that were impaled into the ground along the ever ascending route and after a half-hour march in the blazing sunshine we arrived, sweaty and swearing, outside a medieval ruin of a house to which was attached a dicey-looking barn. Inside were the headquarters of his thriving business.

'*Saluts! Les musiciens!*' called the voice of Monsieur Rafting from among the cobwebs and bats in the dark interior of the barn. We looked around for some musicians, but, finding none, deduced that he was merely addressing us with some irony.

'*Salut, monsieur,*' I said, bravely stepping inside through a gap where part of the wall used to be.

'I think this is the door over here,' said Alastair.

'No, it's this,' said Paul, touching a panel of ancient oak, the crevices of which contained dormant spores of the Black Death dating from the fourteenth century. I heard it creak open at the same time as I banged my head on a canoe that was suspended from the ceiling. There were six other canoes dangling from the perforated beams above me, and to one side of the barn was a stack of about five large inflatable dinghies. As my eyes adjusted to the relative darkness I could see that the walls were littered with ropes, paddles, life jackets and pots of glue – all the essential tools of his business.

'You want to come rafting tomorrow?' asked Monsieur Rafting.

'Well, we thought we might go today if possible,' I replied, looking at all the unused gear around us.

'I'm sorry. I am building my house today. Would you like to see it?'

We followed him through a doorway into the kitchen of the old house. The room was decorated with bare electrical wires protruding from the wall, one of which was connected to a kettle with only black tape to seal the join. A low-wattage light bulb dangled from another wire in the ceiling, also attached with tape. We all ducked under another live ceiling wire which had yet to be professionally attached to something with what was left of his black tape.

'This will be a beautiful kitchen. I will finish it when the summer season ends.'

Two of his children ran past us, pushing and shoving each other and missing some of the exposed wiring by just inches.

'Go and play upstairs,' said Monsieur Rafting in French. The children pushed past us again out of the kitchen and thumped their way upstairs. We followed the kids into a magnificently decrepit hallway that boasted peeling décor dating from the 60s . . . the 1860s. The floor was a mixture of stone flagging and rubble, and we had to step over an assortment of power tools and bags of cement in order to get to the spiral stairs. Halfway up the stairs, as we hopped up over the hole where one of the stone steps used to be, I realised where the rubble in the hallway had come from.

The first floor was a large, open plan playroom/bedroom/building site, criss-crossed with ancient twisted beams. Our host explained how he planned to divide it into various bedrooms and eventually lose the 'building site' décor theme. His children were chasing each other around the enormous room, jumping over missing parts of the floor and somehow missing the many uninsulated electrical wires that had been partially installed all over the place. Monsieur Rafting smiled at them in a relaxed way, then led us back downstairs.

Having seen the rafting king on his home territory I now had no qualms whatsoever about trusting my life to this man on a rafting expedition. If he employed the same high safety standards to his business as he did to his home, there was nothing to worry about.

Nevertheless, we managed to fail to book a trip with him for the next day, preferring instead to head back to town as rapidly as our sweat glands would permit.

★

On the way back towards Castellane we came to a small campsite called Les Lavandes, at which we had never stayed because it wasn't cool enough. The owner of this campsite must have been a founder member of the Hair Bear Bunch in the seventies, but with the onset of his middle age the wild, grey afro hair reaching out-wards from the sides and back of his head now con-trasted sharply with the shiny bald dome on the top. It would be difficult to develop a more mad appearance without actually growing a Belgian moustacheless beard.

The reception hut at Les Lavandes was plastered with posters announcing forms of entertainment that ranged from nature study walks to the local nightclub's competition to find the biggest tits in the region. There were also events taking place on this little campsite, including musical recitals and visiting bands.

'I hate the bloody Automat,' Alastair reminded us. 'He's a tosser.'

'He's stealing all our bloody money,' I added, 'albeit from people who haven't given it to us yet.'

'Why don't we try to get a gig here on this campsite so that we don't have to look at his ugly face tonight?' suggested Paul.

'I won't play here for anything less than a free pizza,' I objected, as I walked into the reception hut and rang the bell.

No one appeared to be inside, and no one could hear the little bell outside.

'Have you seen this poster, guys?' asked Alastair. He pointed to the wall on which was a large photo of a Swedish sauna full of naked Swedes and a tariff underneath. 'There's a naughty sauna on the site.'

'Full of naked Swedes,' I pointed out.

'That's where he'll be, then,' said Paul. 'It must be worth checking out.'

The campsite filled a rectangular patch of land, just a hundred yards wide and exactly the same in dimensions as the Catholic graveyard next door. Noisy neighbours were obviously not a problem for these campers. It had previously been an agricultural field, and was nostalgically decorated with a few sharp, rusty farming implements around the children's play area.

We walked down the central track, looking behind caravans, tents and fat Belgians for the elusive sauna. We found the tiny Swedish structure in the far corner of the site, tucked away behind the canoe shed. There was a window in the pine door, but it was completely steamed up inside. Alastair bravely knocked on the door. We stood back, unsure how angry the occupants would be. If smelly buskers had interrupted my relaxing sauna, I know I wouldn't be too chuffed.

The door swung open with a huge waft of steam that moistened our faces like a hot towel after a curry. From the cloud emerged a hairy leg, then another, then the rest of the Hair Bear's body, loosely covered by a cloth around his waist. I recognised him instantly by the crazy hair.

'*Ah, Simon et Garfunkel!*' he called, jovially. '*Er, et Demis Roussos.*'

Paul was the first to recover from the shock of the inappropriateness of his joy at seeing us.

'*Monsieur Hair Bear,*' said Paul, not quite using those words, '*nous voulons jouer ici ce soir pour les campeurs. A côté des dangereux machines agruculturels.*'

Before Monsieur Hair Bear could answer, however, the door to the sauna opened again and out stepped a teenage Dutch girl, wearing only bikini bottoms and clutching a damp T-shirt to her naked chest. I had scarcely come-to and picked myself up off the ground when another topless girl emerged from the tiny sauna. They both skipped off to their caravans without saying a word to us. Why bother to learn fifteen major languages by the age of twelve if you're not going to speak to us, I wondered?

'You want to sing here tonight in the children's play area, then?' asked the Hair Bear in the kind of impeccable English foreigners manage to learn when they sleep with our wives. He tightened his loin-cloth.

'Yes. You've seen us play in town, I think. We could play for your campers this evening,' continued Paul.

'I can't pay much. How about seven hundred Francs for an hour?'

It was enough for fourteen pizzas, so I was happy with the deal. Alastair had a better idea, though.

'And we can still pass the hat around?'

'Of course you can,' replied the Hair Bear. 'And you will eat here as my guests before the show.'

I could sense that Paul was having trouble coping with someone as utterly insane as this. He was offering to give away substantial amounts of food and money to three untalented beggars in return for some painfully speeded-up renditions of *Mrs Robinson* and *Hey Jude*.

'Shall I call a psychiatrist for him?' whispered Paul.

'Or a hairdresser?' suggested Alastair.

'We'll see you tonight, then. About seven,' I said. '*Au revoir, musiciens.*'

*

The prospect of having to produce a suitably professional performance for a paid gig loomed over our heads all afternoon like a really big hat, blotting out the sun. But no matter what level of humiliation we were to experience that night, at least we could be certain of avoiding the bloody Automat. In any case, we opted to reduce the chances of being booed off the campsite by actually rehearsing our act for a change. There were little song lists sellotaped to the tops of our guitars: these contained enough songs for three busking sets of about fifteen minutes each. The first set contained the stuff we knew well and played every day. The second set could be done in an emergency, and the third consisted entirely of songs we thought it would be cool to play but which we were too lazy ever to learn.

None of us had given any thought as to whether we could produce the requested hour of muzak. I could juggle a bit, but would usually drop my balls after a few seconds. There were just two options open to us: play our songs more slowly, roughly akin to their normal

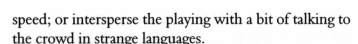

speed; or intersperse the playing with a bit of talking to the crowd in strange languages.

'*Ghhhkhhshhhpppooodle erschtkirscheplops,*' would usually generate applause from the Dutch community, pleased that someone had learned to say good evening in their language. We could also say *please, thank you,* and *nice daughters mate* in Dutch. Another useful phrase was,

'*N'avez pas peur de notre chapeau. Il a faim, mais il ne mange jamais les enfants!*' which loosely translated as *give us all your money, you French bastards.*

There was a limit to how often we could repeat these rather crap phrases, however, so an unprecedented slowing down of the songs would have to be attempted.

The looming hat grew bigger and heavier.

★

Cheap photocopied posters were plastered all over the campsite when we arrived, announcing the imminent arrival of a group called, imaginatively, *Les Chanteurs.* They were due to be singing at the same time as us.

'We must be the support group,' said Paul, with much relief.

'*Les Chanteurs!*' shouted the Hair Bear, emerging from his office. '*Et Monsieur Creosote!*' he added, so that Paul would not feel left out. 'Put your guitars inside. You will eat with us before you sing.'

Our instruments were wrenched from us by his eager little assistants, dressed in torn T-shirts and dripping from a recent water pistol fight amongst the rusty blades of the old farm equipment. An odd smell hung in the air, apparently from the direction of the barbecue. It was an unpleasant stench, like burning tar or Brussells railway station.

'Smells like they're barbecuing one of their canoes,' I warned the others.

The Hair Bear had put one of his minions in charge of the cooking, and he seemed unflustered by the apparently weird results.

'I am letting my toilet cleaner cook tonight,' he told us proudly, without a hint of trepidation in his voice.

'Oh good,' lied Paul.

'Normally he likes to put his arm inside blocked waste pipes to see what is causing the problem. The thrill of discovery gives him great job satisfaction.'

'Oh good,' lied Alastair.

'Yesterday he found a ring. He's wearing it now.'

'Oh good,' I lied.

'Usually he finds what we call *po-po*,' explained the Hair Bear. 'He puts it over there.' He pointed to a steaming compost heap next to the little pizzeria caravan. '*Stephan, viens-ici! Je te presente les chanteurs*.' The Hair Bear beckoned the toilet cleaner towards our table.

Smoke began to build up around the barbecue the moment the toilet cleaner turned his back on it, but no one seemed to mind. Stephan was cooking on half an oil drum, but he hadn't removed much of the oil first. As the barbecue heated up, the smoke from the burning oil became thicker and smellier, occasionally wafting into our nostrils and staying there.

The Hair Bear stood up and loudly introduced his most trusted and valuable employee to us. We stood up

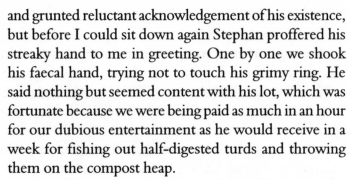

and grunted reluctant acknowledgement of his existence, but before I could sit down again Stephan proffered his streaky hand to me in greeting. One by one we shook his faecal hand, trying not to touch his grimy ring. He said nothing but seemed content with his lot, which was fortunate because we were being paid as much in an hour for our dubious entertainment as he would receive in a week for fishing out half-digested turds and throwing them on the compost heap.

The toilet cleaner returned and wafted away the smoke, picked some blackened items off the barbecue and threw them onto a row of dusty plates. He then brought them over and served us first, as honoured guests. My plate proudly boasted a steak garnished with herbs and Mobil. The Hair Bear wibbled ebulliently throughout the meal about his sauna, his antique farming implements, and about the good old days when his hairstyle had been fashionable, but we weren't paying attention; were too busy trying to chew the crude oil we had been served.

When he had finished pushing back the culinary boundaries of engine oil and meat, the toilet cleaner poured water onto the barbecue, causing a plume of steam to rise high into the evening sky. He then wandered back to the toilet block to see what new discoveries he could make underneath the Ladies.

'Would you like dessert, *musiciens*?' asked the Hair Bear. 'And Paul? Stephan will bring you some ice cream if you like.'

'I think we should start playing now, before the dessert comes,' I suggested. 'The campsite is full to bursting with people at the moment, but they'll want to go out soon and find some entertainment if we don't hurry.'

The gig started off badly, then went into something of a decline. I announced the first song as *Bye Bye Love*, which Alastair loyally started singing, but I got distracted by a passing breast and started singing *Eight Days A Week* instead. The only continuity was Paul's bassline, which didn't distinguish between songs anyway. His note could accompany any piece of popular music. Nevertheless, the song was abandoned and we started again.

The next song was *I Saw Her Standing There*, a lively ditty designed to get even the stiffest hips in the audience gyrating. Tonight, however, this song was also abandoned early because one of my guitar strings went *ping* and snapped as I played the intro with excessive gusto. I scrabbled around in my guitar bag for a replacement G-string, and put it on in front of the ever-growing, curious, audience. By the time I had tuned it up there was about a hundred people gathered to see us. Some had brought their own chairs from their caravans, and were seating themselves in a semi-circle around us; others were standing behind them. We started the song again and roughly bodged our way through to the end of it, where we were met by rapturous applause. How odd.

To change the mood a little we sang a couple of love songs flatly and without any feeling, sensitivity or passion whatsoever. They loved it. We then reverted to rock 'n' roll with a solo-less and soulless rendition of *Long Tall Sally*, the end of which Alastair managed to reach a full twelve bars ahead of the rest of us, such was his superior musical ability. They went wild. When we tried *Hotel*

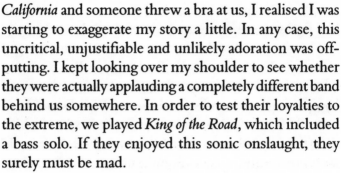

California and someone threw a bra at us, I realised I was starting to exaggerate my story a little. In any case, this uncritical, unjustifiable and unlikely adoration was off-putting. I kept looking over my shoulder to see whether they were actually applauding a completely different band behind us somewhere. In order to test their loyalties to the extreme, we played *King of the Road*, which included a bass solo. If they enjoyed this sonic onslaught, they surely must be mad.

'Do you have a tape we could buy?' called a nearby Dutch voice during the standing ovation (albeit due to insufficient seats). Perhaps they had all just been released from an isolated monastery after a Spartan decade of candle-making, brass rubbing and masturbation? This was the only reason I could think of for their behaviour, other than that they were applauding us with heavy irony, which was unlikely given the preponderance of Belgians.

After the gig, the Hair Bear produced a thick wad of notes, totalling a hundred Francs more than he had originally promised. The voluntary donations from the crowd almost doubled our undeserved takings. Earning this money didn't seem right. It had been too easy, as if we had taken advantage of an audience who didn't know any better. It had required as much skill on out part as passing a driving test in Belgium (which mostly consists of being able to tune the radio into the most bizarre rock 'n' roll pipe organ stations whilst not looking where you're going). Even Stephan put some grimy coins of indeterminate currency into our hat.

'Will you come back and play again next week?' asked the Hair Bear as we prepared to leave with our ill-gotten gains.

'Sorry, but the rest of Europe is crying out to be entertained by our own peculiar brand of rock 'n' roll,' I explained.

'And if they're not crying now they soon will be once we've passed through,' added Paul. 'Besides, I've got to get home for my sister's wedding at the weekend, then we're meeting up again in Paris ready to start some full speed Inter-Railing.'

'That is a shame,' said the Hair Bear. 'You are very talented musicians,' he added, looking at myself and Alastair. 'And you,' he said, looking at Paul, 'you have very nice shoes.'

– Mad Madge's
Whitewater Adventure –

Paul

As it was my penultimate day in Castellane, the others had decided that we should do something stupid for old times' sake. Needless to say, this idea appealed to me no end but, sadly, the vision of the others had not extended to tracked vehicles with guns, medieval siege weapons, the hurling of rotten vegetables from an elevated position of the town or anything near as puerile. The fact that we had been unable to go rafting yesterday and that today the Verdon was at such a low flow as to make rafting impossible was not allowed to scotch our enthusiasm to do something insane. Back at the campsite we discussed what other options for stupid activity existed in the immediate vicinity. Alastair emerged from behind his dog-eared Wilbur Smith novel with an idea.

'We could go rafting without rafts?'

'Er, yes. How would we go about that then?' I countered.

'Rafts are for girls,' declared Alastair.

'Yeah, and so are climbing harnesses,' enthused Stewart helpfully, 'and tampons.'

'We can use our lard to raft on. You're fat enough to float well and if you're pounded against the rocks your blubber will absorb the force,' added Alastair thought-fully. He had a point. With a minimal amount of planning, and after we had packed some essential supplies like cigarettes, chocolate and towels, we set off up the road towards where we thought the action might be. Stewart brought some Elastoplast in case we injured ourselves.

The road led upwards as did all the roads out of Castellane. This one in particular held a few memories for us as it was a mile or so down this road that we had stayed (briefly) on our very first Inter-Rail trip when we were sprightly and gangly seventeen year-olds. Also down this road were numerous, second rate campsites, the names of which I cannot disclose here in case a single copy of this book ever makes it back to Castellane. Back in those days we would do anything to avoid walking the mile or so into town but today we were glad of the exercise – Alastair's comments, although not exactly from the mouth of an Adonis, had made me self-conscious. I wasn't sweating like a fat bloke though, so that was all right.

The road clung tightly to the bottom of the mountains. Sheer limestone cliffs rose up on our right while the road dropped away to the river on our left. Sometimes the drop was only a few feet (and probably survivable in a car providing one wasn't driving anything Italian) to fifty feet where the road rose sharply away from the water. This was a bloody dangerous road by anyone's standards: anyone, that is, except a Frenchman. If you're French you only need one piece of safety equipment to guarantee you safe passage along the roads of *Gorges du Verdon*. 'What is this marvellous accessory?' you are probably asking. A crash helmet? Good tyres? A seatbelt? A five-point racing harness? No, it's a loud horn. That's all you need. Decide to overtake on a blind hairpin bend going up a mountain?

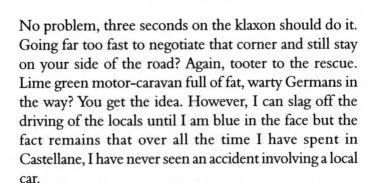

No problem, three seconds on the klaxon should do it. Going far too fast to negotiate that corner and still stay on your side of the road? Again, tooter to the rescue. Lime green motor-caravan full of fat, warty Germans in the way? You get the idea. However, I can slag off the driving of the locals until I am blue in the face but the fact remains that over all the time I have spent in Castellane, I have never seen an accident involving a local car.

★

We stopped at a gravelled lay-by just ahead of a precarious-looking rock outcrop that hung out over the road promising, but never actually managing, to do something useful like collapse on the caravan parked there, attached to a rusty, ten-year old, British-registered Montego. Thankfully, for both parties, our arrival coincided with their departure. We scrambled down the loose stones of the steep bank and stood watching the river. It looked dangerous all of a sudden in the same way that the five metre diving board at swimming pools looks like an absolute doddle until you're actually standing on it, farting nervously through your trunks and trying to formulate an excuse for not diving that won't make you out to be an utter pussy. The river ran quite fast here as the banks of the river were much closer to each other now than on the stretch we had walked up. The tips of several rocks protruded through the turbulent surface hiding their jagged lower parts which would probably cut our legs to ribbons if we were to collide with them. Not for the first time on an Inter-Rail trip I began to feel that foolhardiness and bravado had come before common sense and rational thinking. Still, that's what Inter-Rail is all about I tried to reassure myself.

'I'll set up the resuscitation base over here,' declared Stewart as he clambered onto a dry, safe-looking rock on which he could sunbathe in comfort as we were dragged though the eddying waters like flotsam and jetsam. 'There's chocolate available for energy if you want it.'

I turned back to look at the water and my mind turned to a college project we'd had to do. The project was to design a river management system for the river Dee from its source near Bala in Wales all the way to the Irish Sea. The system would use predictive technologies, sluices, weirs, flumes and reservoirs to manage the water so effectively that wholesale flooding of Chester could be achieved, if necessary, at the push of a button. The knowledge gained from the fluid mechanics side of this project would give me an advantage in knowing where to enter the river and what course to follow, should I actually be able to control my direction, once I was in. The problem was, however, that I had done the software and communications side of the project and left the difficult mathematics and Reynolds numbers to Fletch – a fellow student – as he was a proper engineer. Bollocks, I was doomed. Alastair's voice shouted at me over the noise of the water.

'Got your safety gear mate?' I looked at him to see that he had secured his recently acquired copper colander to his head with string and was wearing it as a crash helmet. The situation became surreal as I looked at Alastair.

'Nah. Safety's for lasses and queers, mate!'

With that, Alastair, screaming at the top of his voice, released his handhold on a rock and was immediately swept away. He went out of sight for several seconds before a triumphant but muted, unseen voice yelled,

'I am Mad Madge and I am unsinkable!'

Not wanting to lose face further by procrastinating I also slipped into a jet of fast-running water and was swept away. The sensation was exhilarating and frightening at the same time in much the same way as one's first pillion ride on a motorcycle piloted by a certified psychopath. It was also absolutely freezing. I was washed round a rock and into a still pool where Alastair was treading water.

'Do it again?' he panted.

'Let's quit while we're ahead.'

'. . . or while we've still got a head.' With that Alastair swam off towards the bank singing about being mad. I followed, quietly agreeing with him.

★

Back on Stewart's resuscitation rock an hour or so later we decided to make our way back to Monsieur Mistral's. Alastair was still in a state of excitement on the way home.

'I reckon we should get some bangers and let them off somewhere,' he suggested.

'Yeah, like at the chapel on top of the rock,' I ventured.

Stewart had his reservations.

'That might be dangerous and get us into trouble with Monsieur Moustache.'

'What would Wilbur Smith do with bangers?' I asked.

'If it was Wilbur they'd be sticks of dynamite, not bangers and he's be using them to blast a path through some rock to find the missing diamonds, I expect.' Alastair paused for breath. 'However, in this case, in the south of France, he'd probably drive along the mountain roads in a Maserati convertible, lighting the fuses with a smouldering Montecristo cigar and toss them into Camp du Verdon where they would tear asunder all those in a fifty foot radius. Or something like that.'

'Hmm,' I mused, 'but, bearing in mind we have no car, open topped or otherwise, no cigar and no desire to kill anyone as we probably wouldn't get away with it, we'll have to settle for something less extravagant.'

Alastair was full of enthusiasm and, unwilling to let this enthusiasm wane, we set off to a shop in town that we hoped might sell the explosives we were looking for.

As we walked into town I tried to come up with a legitimate reason to want bangers. What purpose did they serve apart from exploding frogs, breaking milk bottles and startling everyone in earshot? I couldn't come up with a plausible answer in the time it took us to reach the dramatically-named 'Safari' – purveyor of compasses, tarpaulins and fishing rods, among other things.

'You ask for them,' prompted Alastair as we looked through the window at a display of bait tubs.

'I don't even know what the word for banger is.'

'I think it's *pétard* or something. Go on, mate.'

I refused to do it on the grounds that I had no confidence of Alastair's recollection of the word for banger. This established we entered the shop.

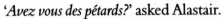

'*Avez vous des pétards?*' asked Alastair.

Monsieur Safari eyed him suspiciously. I was right: Alastair had just asked for an enema or something and now Monsieur Safari was going to eviscerate him with one of his hunting knives.

'*Des pétards?*' he checked. Alastair looked at me, exasperated.

'*Oui,*' he added hesitantly. Alastair also thought that this would be a good time for some sign language so in his right hand he clutched an invisible hand grenade while his left hand removed the invisible pin. Then he hurled the invisible weapon behind Monsieur Safari's counter while making the appropriate sound effects (including the explosion).

Monsieur Safari looked distinctly unimpressed by this little tirade and, putting his hands on his hips and glaring at us both, he simply said;

'*Non!*'

Helpfully, he pointed at us both and then at the door. I think he was probably out of stock.

– A Horse's Wanger
Covered In Icing Sugar –

PAUL

I left Castellane early on Thursday morning on the rickety Chemins de Fer de Provence. This particular transport system did not inspire confidence but, I assured myself, as I was on a southbound journey of which ninety percent was downhill, the chances of us breaking down were slim. The journey towards the more professionally run SNCF station at Nice was a picturesque but uneventful affair, the most amusing incident being the train driver's failure to notice a group of people at a request stop in the middle of nowhere. I watched in amusement as the train rumbled past the stranded passengers, theirs mouths wide in disbelief, and finally stopped about quarter of a mile too late. Eventually realising that the driver had no intention of wasting precious diesel by reversing back up the hill to the station, the marooned crowd reluctantly jogged down the tracks dragging their luggage behind them.

The first thing I did on arriving at Nice was to verify the time of departure for trains from Marseille to Paris. I hauled my shit and myself over to the information kiosk with the shortest queue and waited. As the foregoing passengers in the queue were dealt with in typical southern French unconcern, I began to worry about missing my connecting train. I kept looking up at the wall clock, making a fresh mental calculation with every glance. To my relief I was soon at the head of the queue. I asked the information fascist when the trains left

Marseille. The Oracle, who had sold us our Inter-Rail tickets back at his shiny travel information centre and who knew the entire European timetable by heart, would have been appalled by the fact that his French counterpart had not committed every train's movements for the coming season to memory. As I considered the chastising *Monsieur Informatique* would get from the Oracle for his complacency, the French kiosk bloke shuffled over to a big pile of books on a trolley behind him. I expected him to pick one up and bring it back to me but no, this was not to be the case. Now that I wasn't facing him, he decided that this would be a good time for a *Gauloise*.

He plucked a cigarette from his shirt pocket, straightened it out and lit it. The cigarette immediately sagged under its own weight, such is the quality of French fags. At this point I expected him maybe to have one drag, select a timetable and wander back over to his desk but this was obviously one of those special moments for him and I watched, dumbstruck, as he merely propped himself up on the trolley and continued to take leisurely puffs. This display of inertia and indifference prompted me to have a cigarette too so I withdrew a Marlboro and joined the fucker at his own game. At least this way, I thought, he'd finish before me.

Eventually, as if requiring all of his available willpower and strength, the helpful SNCF employee did what I had been willing him to do for the last three or four minutes. He returned to his desk and dropped the book down in front of me. Then, without even opening it, he informed me that the train would leave at two minutes to two. I would also need to make a reservation even to be considered for passage on anything as prestigious as the TGV, he added. Thirty-five Francs poorer and pretty pissed off by the 'service' I had received I left the bizarrely named 'Help Office' and made my way to the platform to await my connecting train to Marseille.

The train to Marseille was a standard one. By this I mean that it surpassed anything I had previously seen in England that was designated First Class. I took up a seat by a table and began to disengage my brain in readiness for the two-hour voyage. I was soon joined by Jim Morrison from The Doors. He was less fat, less dead and decidedly more French than I remembered him but he seemed friendly enough so we started talking.

As the train ground its way along the Riviera, Jim told me he was going to visit his daughter at a place near Marseille. This revelation was fascinating, as I'm sure you'll agree, and I reacted to it with the response it warranted – i.e. nothing. Jim was a friendly soul, however, so I offered him a cigarette and we sat chatting about diverse and exciting topics that encompassed his recent unemployment, an old Triumph (or 'Treeeomf') Dolomite he had once owned and how it was now lunchtime. With this he rummaged around in his bag and withdrew an example of my most hated item of French cuisine – the dusty sausage. I shuddered as I saw him take a grotesquely huge bite from what I can only describe as a horse's wanger covered in icing sugar. To my horror he then offered me a bite. In the cross section of the sausage I could see huge lumps of fat, gristle and what appeared to be string. Lying, I told him that I was a vegetarian. Being French he didn't understand this concept at all so I had to explain it to him.

After our uneasy lunchtime, during which Jim failed to come to terms with the concept of life without eating animals, our discussions continued. He asked where I was going so I told him that I was returning to England after only two weeks in France to attend my eldest sister's wedding. As I reached the end of that sentence I realised that I didn't actually know the French word for wedding so I said that my sister had a marriage, making the 'marriage' sound as Gallic as possible. Jim seemed to understand so I assumed I had made a lucky guess. Alas, my lifelong friendship with Jim was brought to a premature end as Marseille station edged into view.

The TGV was already at the station on an adjacent platform when I arrived. Peering though the tinted windows as I ambled up the platform, the train appeared to be very full. I'd be all right though – I had a reservation.

Finding no obvious helpful information printed on my reservation ticket I sought assistance from a nearby fascist.

'Monsieur, je ne peut pas voir sur cette billet, un numéro pour mon siège,' I explained. The fascist looked confused. I thought I'd just told him that I was unable to see a seat number on my ticket. Facing a bemused silence from the fash, I decided to try again. *'Il n'y a pas un numéro, pour l'assiete,'* I pointed through the train window just in case I had mistakenly used the word for 'armadillo' where in fact I meant 'seat'. A look of realisation crept over the fascist's face.

'Ah, oui!' he exclaimed.

'At last,' I thought – communication has been established.

'*Ça,*' he said, pointing at my reservation, '*ça c'est un reservation!*'

'Well done,' I thought 'no wonder you're in the travel business – you really know your stuff!' I expected him to give me some more pearls of wisdom but none seemed to be forthcoming.

'*Oui, je sais qu'il est un reservation, je l'ai acheté moi-même, mais où est le nombre pour le siège?*' I asked, exasperated. It was just like talking to the muppets back in England only smellier.

The fash went on to explain, using several words I had never before heard, that a reservation was indeed obligatory to travel on the TGV but it didn't entitle you to a seat. The whole situation just slipped from my grasp at this point. If the TGV carries, say, 1000 people, surely there would only be 1000 reservations possible for any one journey and one would therefore stop selling once the thousandth one had been sold. This was clearly not the case though, and as I began mentally to prepare an intricate sentence in French to propose this theory to the fascist he added,

'*On peut s'asseyer là-bas,*' pointing to an open door in the train. Dejectedly, I slipped through it.

On board France's pride and joy the only available perch was the baggage space between two carriages. Resignedly, I folded a seat out of the train wall and realised I hadn't brought any drink with me. I lit a fag instead and morosely considered the four hour journey ahead of me.

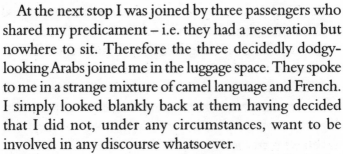

At the next stop I was joined by three passengers who shared my predicament – i.e. they had a reservation but nowhere to sit. Therefore the three decidedly dodgy-looking Arabs joined me in the luggage space. They spoke to me in a strange mixture of camel language and French. I simply looked blankly back at them having decided that I did not, under any circumstances, want to be involved in any discourse whatsoever.

The Arabs started drinking what smelled like turpentine from a bottle concealed in a paper bag. At least they balanced out their intake with multiple bags of chipsticks. My mum would have been happy – she always stressed the importance of a balanced diet.

About twenty miles outside of Paris the driver crackled over the tannoy that the train would be late arriving in Paris. I was a little unnerved by this revelation: I had not allowed a great amount of time for my connection between Gare Saint Lazare and Gare du Nord.

A few moments later the train stopped moving completely. Now, I'm not sure about other people but this is one aspect of train travel that really pisses me off. It's probably a personal niggle (of which I have thousands) but I would rather be edging forward at two miles an hour for ten minutes than stationary for nine and a half minutes and then moving at normal speed for the remaining thirty seconds.

I surfaced from the *Metropolitain* to find myself in a city street. This was much more open-air than I had remembered the station to be. Seeing a nearby prostitute I ran up to her and asked for directions to the station. Reluctantly she pointed to her left and mumbled something past her cigarette. I didn't catch what she said – I was sprinting for the station.

Inside the grandiose building I took a couple of seconds to scan the departures board. There was a train bound for Le Havre. I didn't even check to see when it was due to depart, I simply darted along the concourse looking for the right platform. My guitar bounced and wobbled precariously in my grasp while my rucksack jogged up and down on my back enthusiastically. When I reached platform fourteen there was a train there. Without looking to check what its destination might be I flung myself through the open doors and came to a sudden, panting halt outside the carriage toilet. Only two or three seconds later the train's hydraulics hissed into action and the doors were shut.

As I stood, hunched over my baggage, I was aware of several sets of eyes boring into me. I looked up to see several people looking at me intently. I tried to regulate my breathing and compose myself. I stared back at the passengers and, one by one, their eyes drifted back to the papers and magazines they had been reading.

I dumped my rucksack on the floor and sat myself on top of it. I was parched and I began to toy with the idea of drinking some water from the basin in the WC. Luckily, the more sensible part of me decided it would be better in the long run to go without, stagger onwards erratically, eventually collapse and wake up, dazed and confused in a French hospital with an intravenous drip. An elderly man who had been looking at me for a minute or so gradually shuffled his way down the aisle towards me. He was moving so slowly he managed to generate

107

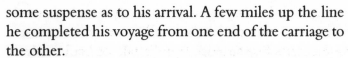

some suspense as to his arrival. A few miles up the line he completed his voyage from one end of the carriage to the other.

'*Bonjour*,' he said, by way of introduction.

'*Salut!*' I replied.

'*T'as soif?*' he enquired.

I thought it would be pretty obvious that I would kill for a drink. As I was thinking this and, as if in some kind of dream, he withdrew a can of beer from his jacket pocket. There had to be a catch. Maybe he wanted to shag me – that's what most strange continental men wanted from me whenever I went abroad. I never could work that out. Uncle Olly always maintained it was my blue eyes but it was a sad fact that wherever I went, I seemed to attract foreign queers.

'*Bien sûr!*' I replied as soon as I was able to compose myself.

The old man seemed friendly enough without being too friendly. He asked me where I was going. I thought it would be fairly obvious – I was English, I had a rucksack and I was on the train that went to the continental ferry port. Still, he was a pleasant chap so I got chatting to him. Then he asked me if I was an American. I felt physically sick at the accusation and had to explain politely that if I were American I would be wearing garish shorts and complaining loudly that there wasn't a goddamn buffet car on the train.

The old bloke apologised for having made such a dreadful *faux pas* and, by way of an excuse, said that he thought only Americans smoked Marlboro, pointing at my cigarette. Having ascertained exactly where we stood regarding our cerebrally-challenged transatlantic counterparts he started relating a tale of his boyhood during the latter days of the war. He used to live in a small town in Normandy which, like most towns, had a river running through it. It was also a supply line for 'le Bosche', he explained. He pulled a face as if he were taking part in some sort of gurning competition. I took that to mean he held the Germans in about as much esteem as I held Americans.

Apparently, the RAF in their 'mustique' fighter-bombers had flown over one day and blown up three out of the four bridges that crossed the river. He then went on to eulogise about the prowess of the British fighting forces and their professionalism. I was finding this very odd as it was coming from a Frenchman. Two days later, the Americans came over to destroy the last bridge but managed not only to miss completely their intended target but also to destroy a quarter of the town and its inhabitants. I sniggered, thinking how typical it was of them to fuck something up in such a big way, until I realised I was also laughing at the unfortunate end of many of his friends and family. Deciding that a change of topic would be prudent, I explained that my sister had a *mariage* in a couple of days and that I had to be present for it. There was no way on Earth I could think of the French word for 'usher' so we left it at that.

I arrived at Le Havre in good time and set off towards the ferry terminal listening to Abba on my walkman – well, it was trendy at the time: that's my excuse.

STEWART

Without Paul's flatulent body clock to wake us up, we slept in until nearly lunchtime. Everyone else in Castellane had already got up and done adventurous things like mountaineering, water-skiing and drinking the local water. By the time I had staggered clumsily to the toilet block and recycled last night's rosé, Monsieur Rafting would have nonchalantly completed three white-water suicide missions down the turbulent Verdon with a paddle in one hand and an interesting magazine in the other. I began my daily hunt to gather from all the campsite cubicles enough virgin toilet paper to cope with a single defecation, and was delighted to find virtually an entire roll in only the second cubicle I visited. It was marked as a ladies' room, but that didn't matter: it just meant the seat wasn't covered in piss.

Having successfully fulfilled all the objectives of the toiletary mission, I stepped out into the blinding daylight and started walking back to the tent to get dressed. Funky music was playing loudly in a nearby Dutch caravan, but it was starting to get drowned out by a loud wailing that seemed to fill the entire Verdon valley, like an air raid siren. Well, like an air raid siren when there's about to be an air raid, obviously; not like one that's just sitting in a box at a car boot sale and nobody really knows what it is and an old lady buys it to use as a flower pot.

Alastair was outside the tent, looking up at the chapel on the rock, which was the source of the siren.

'It's not a Belgian car horn,' he explained, 'it means they're letting water out of the reservoir, so the Verdon will flood. If we're lucky there might be a tidal wave.'

'Cool.'

We spent the afternoon sunbathing in the shade, watching occasional bright red rescue vehicles rushing out from Castellane along the road to emergencies taking place in the gorge. Some of our more depressing neighbours packed up their immaculate brown tents into their pristine, underpowered brown saloon cars and buggered off to have a boring time somewhere else, leaving square patches of brown grass exposed for the first time in days. More rescue vehicles came and went as the afternoon dragged on into evening, and as we sat on the grass doing nothing but providing an adventure playground for ants amongst the hairs on our legs, we felt we might be missing out on something big, like the kind of feeling you get when you hear there's a big party going on next door but no one invited you to it because they all hate you.

There was a definite buzz in the air as we walked into town that evening. I shooed the pesky wasp away and tried to listen in on the conversations of the locals.

'*Mouton . . . vin . . . quatre générations . . . le résistance . . . je me couche avec ma vache . . .*'

The few mumbled words I could understand in isolation from the conversations of the peasants playing pétanque in the main square didn't mean anything, and didn't enlighten me as to the day's events. We decided to head for a bar and interrogate a delicious bar maid.

'Hey guys, wait,' called a throbbingly sexy Dutch voice from behind us.

I turned round to face Wonderwoman, a tower of blonde perfection, with Thierry at her side. Except she

111

wasn't perfect anymore, and neither was her sex-chum. Both of them were covered in cuts, bruises and patches of red anti-septic powder. They looked as if they had spent the day inside a bottle bank followed by a round of paintball.

'What happened?' I asked Wonderwoman's breasts.

'Let's sit down and get some drinks first,' said Thierry.

We sat at Jo-Jo's, by the fountain, and ordered a round of beers. Inside the bar I could see the owner chatting to someone from behind the counter. Then he saw us, and rushed outside to our table, smiling broadly. Our popularity as scrounging buskers was amazing, I started to think. But he didn't acknowledge me at all, nor Alastair.

'*Les héroes de Castellane!*' he announced to all present, pointing at Thierry and Wonderwoman. '*Les bières sont gratuites pour vous.*' He shook their hands as if they were royalty then went back to work.

'This is all very embarrassing,' said Wonderwoman. 'We were just on a hundred kilometre cycle ride in the gorge when the river level suddenly rose and became torrential. We saw two children drowning and we dived in and saved them.'

'We were all swept many kilometres downstream,' continued Thierry. 'The water dragged us over many sharp rocks, and we used our bodies to protect the children from the impacts.'

'Then we carried them to the nearest house where we called in the rescue services,' concluded Wonderwoman. 'I wish people wouldn't make such a big deal out of it. I do this for a living. It was just a typical day at the office for me.'

'It's all rather boring, really,' said Thierry. 'I don't want to keep talking about it. My body hurts at the moment, but that doesn't matter. It will get better. What about you two? What did you do today?'

I didn't like that question. The only truthful answer was that we had sat on our arses all day until they went numb, but I felt that a more energetic story was necessary to make us worthy drinking companions for this Nobel Prize for Good Eggdom winning couple.

'We walked up to the church on the rock,' I lied. 'Then we abseiled down the cliff, and then we did it all again.'

'Really?' asked Wonderwoman in a tone that acted like a truth serum in my veins.

'No, not really. We sat on our arses all day until they went numb.'

Some of the other drinkers around us came over to shake Thierry and Wonderwoman's hands. It was most flattering to be sitting with two such heroic people, but none of their glory seemed to be rubbing off on us. I held my hand out to shake with some of the young ladies who came to congratulate the heroes, but none took up the invitation.

'We will only cycle fifty kilometres tomorrow,' said Thierry. Otherwise our wounds will break open and bleed. Our mountain bikes are expensive, and we don't want to get any more blood on them.'

'It may be uncomfortable when we make love tonight,' warned Wonderwoman. 'I think it would be best if I sit on your penis while you lie on your back. I have the strength to ride you for a couple of hours like that. There will be less pain in that position and you will be able to lick my bosoms.'

We shuffled our feet awkwardly. In one sense, her manners were impeccable – it would have been impolite for her to have discussed her sexual plans for the evening in Dutch so that we wouldn't understand any of it – but at the same time there was nothing in our limited knowledge of etiquette that prepared us for this situation. Thierry seemed oblivious to our discomfort: he had lived in Holland for long enough to be used to this kind of attitude, and besides he was French.

– Fuffoons –

PAUL

The ferry arrived in Portsmouth at an unsavoury hour. Luckily, my mum was used to getting up at unsavoury hours in the morning, such was her role as a mother, so she was there to meet me.

'When was the last time you had a bath, Paul?' she enquired predictably.

'Nineteen eighty-something, I suppose.'

STEWART

Today was the day that *Les Chanteurs* ceased to be the most famous product of Castellane: the story of Thierry and Wonderwoman's heroism had made it onto page two of *Le Sud*. Castellane had never received such recognition before, and was unlikely ever again to raise its obscure head above the Mediterranean parapet in such a way once the hysteria had died down.

We were pig sick of it all. Thierry was breakfasting outside at Jo-Jo's when we arrived for a mid-morning busk, only to find that the bloody Automat had beaten us to it. Thierry was looking healthy and refreshed after a night flat on his back, but he had barely had a chance to begin eating his croissants due to the incessant flow of well-wishers, congratulators and crawly-bumlickers like ourselves who were occupying his valuable time.

'Hey, guys, did you see me in the paper?' asked Thierry. He looked up at us and gave us a smile that said *I shagged Wonderwoman last night and you didn't*. He was wearing a pair of mildly bloodstained shorts and a shirt that was

115

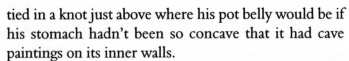
tied in a knot just above where his pot belly would be if his stomach hadn't been so concave that it had cave paintings on its inner walls.

'You're famous today, aren't you?' I observed. 'What's it like?'

'It feels great, you know, like the kind of feeling you get when you're a swimming instructor for a class of teenage Dutch girls who all have a crush on you, and they keep pretending they can't swim so that I have to hold them in the water.'

'Oh, it feels like *that*, does it?'

'It's just cool,' added Thierry. 'You guys should do some exercise some day, you know. You look terrible.'

'Cheers.'

'You wanna come to Lac d'Allos with us today? It's the highest lake in Europe. A bunch of us are going to walk up to it this morning.'

'What about your injuries?'

'Hey, they'll heal better if I keep active. I don't want to end up unfit and flabby like you two. Would you like to come too?'

We hadn't yet made any plans for today, other than a rather sedentary gawping at Dutch girls in the morning and maybe a gawp at some others in the afternoon. It was our penultimate day in Castellane before we headed north to meet Paul in Paris for some seriously inexcusable Inter-Railing, and it seemed a good idea to do something vaguely interesting just in case we ever came to write a book about it. So despite the implication of physical effort in Thierry's words, we were almost tempted. But the sun was hot, the trickle of the fountain was cool, and the prospect of a day spent drinking iced refreshments in the shade whilst dribbling at the sight of scantily-clad young foreign ladies was a stronger magnet to us than a lake so far from civilisation that it didn't even have a caravan site next to it.

'I don't think so. We have a lot of plans for today,' I porkie-pied.

'Wonderwoman will be coming with us. And some of her girlfriends from Holland.'

That put a totally different perspective upon things. If half the girls we wanted to drool at were going on the expedition, then so were we. I looked at Alastair for approval: he was drooling as much as I was at the prospect.

'Well, as it's you Thierry, I suppose we could cancel the parachute jump and the pot-holing. Count us in.'

'Do you know Jean Aveugle? He is a friend of mine. We grew up in Castellane together. He has space in his car, so you must meet him in the main square at twelve. Bring food and drink.'

'How will we know him?'

'He has long blond hair and only one eye. But it is a very good eye. He doesn't wear glasses.'

Parachuting and pot-holing suddenly seemed terribly safe. Even a day spent at Monsieur Rafting's house held fewer dangers than accepting a lift with Blind John in a French bumper car along a mountainous road. The power of Wonderwoman over us was strong that day, however, and our libidos accepted the offer on our behalves.

★

We arrived, laden with Cokes and bottles of Vittel, in the car park just as the sun reached its noonday peak. Blind John was sitting on the bonnet of his battered Peugeot, while his girlfriend, Maria Sourde, was in the front passenger seat. Maria was in her early thirties but her dark skin was already starting to wrinkle from many years of exceeding her EU sunlight quota.

'Hello,' I said to them.

'*Pardon?*' asked Maria.

'Who said that?' asked Blind John, turning around. 'Ah, it's you two. Thierry told me to expect a couple of overweight, unfit English people.'

'Have you been looking for us?' asked Alastair.

John gave him half of a cutting stare.

'*Pardon?*' said Maria.

'Come on, let's go,' said John, opening the back door of his car for us. 'We have many kilometres to drive, and my girlfriend has pains, you know? She is expecting the decorators in soon, I think you say.'

'*Pardon?*'

A car horn parped energetically behind us, signalling that Thierry's love vessel full of blonde Dutch girls was ready to depart. I would have given anything to have travelled in that other car rather than with these strangers, but such is one's lot. Blind John followed Thierry out of Castellane and steered us with predictable enthusiasm and gusto up the twisty mountain roads to Allos. He talked constantly in a combination of French and English that was so perfectly balanced as to be completely incomprehensible both to us and to his girlfriend. Once we were away from the village traffic and travelling at more dangerous speeds, Maria took off her seatbelt, reclined her seat, put her bare feet up on the dashboard and smoked a roll-up with her left arm while dangling the other arm out of the open window. We in the back sat paralysed with fear, holding on to the door handles as tightly as was possible without breaking them.

When we skidded to a halt next to Thierry's car in the dustbowl at the base of Col d'Allos, I felt a sudden direction reversal in my bowel contents as my intense relief sucked in everything that had threatened an untimely and unseemly exit. Thierry and his harem came over to us.

'It is not far to the top,' he reassured the unfit members of the group. Alastair and I nodded our appreciation. 'Just a few hundred metres.' He then explained things in French and Dutch to everyone else.

'*Pardon?*' said Maria.

We weren't wearing any socks today, because we thought we were cool, so any long distance hiking would be impossible. The well-worn hiking boots sported by everyone else didn't worry us at all, nor did the fact that the top of this hill was impossible to see from the car park. The Dutch models set off at a cracking pace, pounding powerfully up the steep and slippery footpath, their blonde hair, sensible walking boots and cute bums quickly disappearing in the distance ahead of us.

Thierry chatted to John and Maria and us for a few metres, then ran up the hill to catch up with the escaping *fuffoons*, shouting,

'We'll stop to smoke some dope half way up. See you there!'

119

We puffed and scuffed and moaned about the incline and tried to think of ways to justify our unfitness and subsequent inability to chat-up the Dutch girls. But there was no excuse for it. In any case, if they were interested in us as playthings they would have slowed down. Then again, they might have been thinking that if we were interested in mounting them, we would have speeded up. My shoes felt loose and sweaty. If I pushed harder my feet just slid around in the goo. Already they were beginning to ache.

'I hope it's going to be downhill on the way back,' I tried to say in French.

'*Pardon?*' said Maria.

The path was busy with frequent clusters of middle-aged walkers, all of whom would pass us no matter which direction they were headed. Even retired war veterans strode past us up the hill so purposefully it seemed as if they were storming Colditz again. It had been some time since we had last seen our Dutch chums in the dim distance: their pre-Raphaelite buns were now replaced with shrivelled military arses.

We were shaded for much of the time by the dense forestry around us, and this enabled me to keep my panting below the socially acceptable level for moral undertakings. The trees grew with less density as we went higher, then as they petered out into open fields spectacular views opened up over distant mountains. Finally the path levelled out across a grassy plain, and I could hear running water nearby.

'Do you hear that?' I asked.

'*Pardon?*'

'Look, there's the others,' said Alastair.

'Where?' asked John.

The others were lying in the grass next to a gurgling stream. They were eating, drinking and smoking suspicious substances. We collapsed in a heap by their sides.

'Did you get lost?' asked Wonderwoman, looking as fresh as if she had just exited a beauty parlour.

'Bit of trouble with the old leg, actually,' I lied, wondering why virtually everything I ever said to Wonderwoman had to be untrue. I pulled off a shoe and let the cool air get to my reddened foot.

'You should get fitter,' she advised me. 'Why don't you have more sex?'

'Good idea. I suppose in Holland you've got gyms with rowing machines next to weight machines next to people who are there to shag you in energetic ways, but unfortunately it's not an option in my local gym. Where's the lake, anyway?'

'We are nearly half way there. The path gets very steep after this field.'

I could hear my feet begging me not to go on, but the Dutch girls had finished their drugs and were preparing for the final ascent. I couldn't give up the chase having come this far, and yet I would be in agony if I didn't rest a bit longer, say for a week or two.

'Wait here while they go to the top,' said my feet. 'You can join them on the way down.'

'No,' said my nob. 'Get to the top with them and they'll probably shag you or go skinny dipping.'

'Ignore your nob,' said my feet. 'You can't walk any further.'

121

'Bollocks,' replied my nob.

'What about them?' asked my feet.

'Nothing. Just bollocks.'

While this epic debate was going on inside me, everyone else had stood up and was ready to move on. I pulled the shoe over my foot.

'Aaaagh!' screamed my foot.

'Phwoarrr!' shouted my nob at the Dutch girls.

I stood up and began the slow, painful ascent to the lake. Everyone walked faster than me and Alastair, but we persevered, silently, steadily, fighting back the pain barrier for a full hour before we reached the brow of the mountain and looked over it. The view we then beheld was the most beautiful sight I had ever seen: the three blonde Dutch girls had stripped off their clothes and were running naked into the lake, splashing and laughing.

'OK,' conceded my injured feet to my nob, 'you win.'

Thierry, Jean and Maria were waiting at the water's edge next to a pile of saucy underwear. The lake was about a hundred feet across, and almost perfectly circular. It was as if we were standing on the edge of an extinct volcano that had filled with water. We were so high up that the flies buzzing around us were of a hardy variety that I had not encountered before, so tough they seemed to be made of iron. The north-facing slope next to the lake was covered with dirty snow, which was a novelty for July, and the east-facing slope was covered with dirty men, namely myself and Alastair, dribbling uncontrollably.

Wonderwoman rose from the water like a goddess, her nipples sharply erect from the effect of the cold water.

She walked over to Thierry and tried to entice him into the water with her, but he was smoking something that he didn't want to get wet.

'You should all come in,' she shouted to us. 'It's beautiful in there.'

'*Pardon?*' said Maria.

'It's beautiful from here, too,' I whispered.

The other two girls chose to get out now, rather than let hypothermia set in. They shivered and shook themselves dry, making no attempt to hide their exquisite womanhoods. We chose this moment to walk over to the assembled party, casually ignoring the fact that three of the world's most beautiful women were naked in our midst.

'Nice day for it,' said Alastair.

Wonderwoman put her white bra and knickers onto her wet body, making them instantly transparent.

'Do you like my body?' she asked Jean.

'It's very nice,' he replied, politely, while she continued to dress.

'I am so glad. I work very hard to stay in good shape. It's nice when people appreciate it.'

'We appreciate it, too,' I said.

'Thank you,' replied Wonderwoman. 'It is a shame you are both in such poor shape, though. You should come to stay with me in Holland some time. I will get you fit in no time at all.'

I didn't know how to react to an invitation like that. It seemed as if we had entered a kind of fantasyland, and that anything was possible, but I couldn't ignore the reality of Thierry standing beside me. It seemed wiser

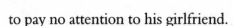
to pay no attention to his girlfriend.

'Aaaargh!' screamed my feet, reminding me of their presence.

I now faced a two hour march with blistered feet and no socks. My shoes were filled with blood by the time we reached the car park again and I feared I would have trouble walking for some days to come. Every step was agony, every small stone on the footpath felt like a needle in my foot. Had it been worth all this pain? Abso-bloody-lutely.

– Nous Buggerons Off –

PAUL

'Get up, you lazy so-and-so,' my grandfather encouraged me while giving me a gentle kick in the ribs.

'Eh?'

'We need those cushions you're sleeping on.'

Of course, the cushions. No-one, no matter how hardy, would endure breakfast sitting only on the plastic garden furniture, so I naturally agreed that it was entirely justifiable to wake me at seven-thirty to reclaim the mattress I was sleeping on. So, today was my sister's big day. She didn't look nervous, but then I'd never seen any other brides directly before their nuptials. She had obviously decided that I had matured over recent years as she had appointed me as an usher at the church. Oooh, the responsibility of it all. What if I dropped a hymn book or accidentally directed someone to the wrong side of the church? It didn't bear thinking about, so I put my concerns behind me and started decking myself out in full-on wedding regalia. Kirstie was getting married at a pleasant village church that she had never attended before, five miles from her house. The ceremony was to be held there before everybody piled back to my parents' gaff to throw wine and food down their gullets until my parents were bankrupt. Much like any other wedding in fact.

Outside, Barrymore, my father's best mate and all-round good egg, was polishing the last part of the jet black Audi that would be taking Kirstie to the church.

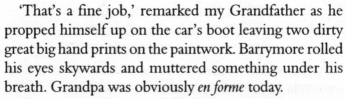

'That's a fine job,' remarked my Grandfather as he propped himself up on the car's boot leaving two dirty great big hand prints on the paintwork. Barrymore rolled his eyes skywards and muttered something under his breath. Grandpa was obviously *en forme* today.

The wedding was much like any other wedding: lots of people purporting to be part of your family but who you don't recognise, the most hideously ostentatious women's hat competition and those pseudo-friends of my parents who they felt they had to invite rather than wanted to invite. I made a mental note that this would not happen, should I ever get married. Still, irony is a cruel thing isn't it?

Back at Chateau Bassett, the reception kicked off in a marquee in the back garden. The marquee looked better in real life than I had imagined it, though my parents' garden wasn't really cut out for functions like this: its size meant that the marquee encompassed some flowerbeds and the patio. Still, no one was going to notice that when there was a tone deaf pianist with no sense of rhythm serenading the guests as they arrived. Maybe this was all a part of a cunning plan by my parents to put all the guests off their food with this cacophonic apparition so that the catering budget could be reduced. Speaking of catering, I took this opportunity to gorge myself thoroughly on food that I knew would not yield any nasty surprises midway through digestion. There was loads of food too, so I made a note to steal what was left over and take it back to France with me.

At around eight o'clock my sister and my new brother-in-law made their excuses and went down to the pub to

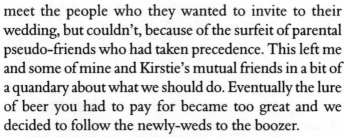

meet the people who they wanted to invite to their wedding, but couldn't, because of the surfeit of parental pseudo-friends who had taken precedence. This left me and some of mine and Kirstie's mutual friends in a bit of a quandary about what we should do. Eventually the lure of beer you had to pay for became too great and we decided to follow the newly-weds to the boozer.

I didn't much like the wedding togs I was wearing and managed to effect a quick Clark Kent-style transformation from Usherman to Normalbloke. I decided to wear the morning coat over my T-shirt and jeans, as I wanted to get my money's worth out of it before it went back to Moss Bros. Down at the pub I found my new brother-in-law and his mates in the beer garden. As if involved in some kind of weird ritual the men were taking it in turns to clamber onto a coal bunker, drop their trousers and mime along to the music that was coming from inside the pub. It seemed a pointless but amusing pastime, so I stood back and observed as I waited my turn on the bunker.

When I returned home the house was full of guests and my room was definitely off-limits. Not wanting another rude awakening at the hands of my grandfather I crept under a trestle table in the marquee and dozed off. The logic to this move was sound but what I could not predict was that my parents' friends would be up at seven the next morning collecting bottles and generally making a racket in the tent. Still, shit happens.

STEWART

The campsite upon which we had been squatting had an indecipherable tariff posted up by its entrance. It was

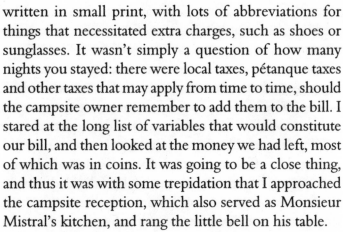

written in small print, with lots of abbreviations for things that necessitated extra charges, such as shoes or sunglasses. It wasn't simply a question of how many nights you stayed: there were local taxes, pétanque taxes and other taxes that may apply from time to time, should the campsite owner remember to add them to the bill. I stared at the long list of variables that would constitute our bill, and then looked at the money we had left, most of which was in coins. It was going to be a close thing, and thus it was with some trepidation that I approached the campsite reception, which also served as Monsieur Mistral's kitchen, and rang the little bell on his table.

'*Ah, Fereeee Stewaaaart,*' he exclaimed, emerging from round the corner. '*Vive la reine!*'

'Indeed. Yes.'

'*Vous partez?*' he mumbled, causing the soggy cigarette in his mouth to wobble slightly.

I nodded to the affirmative and explained that we planned to leave early next morning. He rummaged in his card file and pulled out the details for *Fereeee Stewaaaart* while I held my money bag tightly, desperately hoping I had enough. Interminable seconds passed while he computed complicated campsite algorithms on his abacus. The money bag started to slip in my sweaty palms.

Finally he wrote down an indecipherable figure at the bottom of my card, and I started to tip some coins onto his desk.

'*Non*, is good,' he said, flashing a rare smile in my direction.

I pushed the whole money bag towards him politely, but he brushed it aside. I didn't know which would have been the more embarrassing: being told I didn't have enough money or being told I was valued so much as a guest (despite the damage I caused every year to his fence, grass and waste pipe system) that he didn't want me to pay at all. He may have been a completely mad old peasant, but he had proved himself to be a very generous mad old peasant. I shook his crispy hand and thanked him profusely before returning to the tent to tell Alastair of our good fortune.

'We had enough to pay the bill,' I told him.

'Great. How much is there left?'

'All of it. He hasn't charged us.'

'What a *bon oeuf*. Let's go and spend it in town, then.'

The coins were divided equally between us, the tent was zipped up and we set off for our final walk into town before tomorrow's early departure. Passing Monsieur Mistral's kitchen, however, we were taken aback by the sound of his wife's voice ranting and raving in a full-blown attack on the poor old man. She stepped outside briefly and glared at us, then went back in to continue laying into her husband. I couldn't understand what she was saying, but it was obvious that she didn't approve of him letting us stay for free. I guessed that the entire complicated tariff had been devised by her scheming business brain in the first place, and that poor Monsieur Mistral was valued by her for his bin-emptying prowess rather than for his financial acumen.

We scarpered before she made him change his mind, vowing only to return under cover of darkness. In the meantime we had the task of spreading the cheery news to everyone that we were leaving Castellane for another year, not that any of them gave a bag of monkey's nuts anyway. 'Uh,' was the response of all the restaurant and bar owners, except Jean-Noel at La Main A La Pâte, who simply said, '*En forme?*'

Elien was sorry to see us leave, as always, but the other waitresses seemed no more bothered by the whole thing than were the local stray cats.

We stopped at Jo-Jo's for a couple of hours to make sure it was fully dark before we went back, drinking glass after glass of cheap rosé and talking about how great it would be if we could buy an apartment in one of the crumbling medieval buildings around the little square so that we wouldn't have to share a tent on a campsite run by a man who was so insane that he didn't even want our money.

Staggering homewards we encountered a sudden *brouillard*. It was so dense that I tripped over Eva at the centre of it, making her spill some of her bananas.

'*Ça va?*' she asked, blowing away her cigarette smoke.

'*Oui,*' I said, choking slightly.

'*Je cherche les bébés,*' she said, indicating the fruit in her bag.

So she was still hanging out with those pathetic adolescent, weasel-faced, micro-nobbed, French turds that she called 'the babies'. There really had been no point in trying to compete for Eva's attentions up against gentlemen of such calibre. I was quite glad to be able to tell her, in my best Franglais, that we were leaving the next day.

'*Nous buggerons off demain,*' I declared.

'I am a talentless, tone-deaf bassist (if you'll pardon the tautology), Stewart possesses a strumming style that is so wooden you could make furniture out of it and Alastair, although saddled with perfect pitch and a slightly more rock 'n' roll voice, can't remember lyrics or refrain from creating his own time signatures.'

Some of the more developed parts of Castellane:

Monsieur Mistral

'Des moutons!' Monsieur Mistral observed as if I had never seen sheep before.
'Oui, je sais,' I replied irritably.
'Il y a des moutons en Angleterre?' he asked. I explained that we did indeed have sheep in England but the reason he was unaware of their existence was that most of them seemed to end up consumed by fire at some French roadblock or other in Normandy before they had a chance to get any further inland.

Des moutons.

Route Napoleon bridge, Castellane.

'Why Napoleon was looking for a campsite near Castellane isn't clear, and why he should be honoured for it I have no idea. If it's a military connection, how come there's no Route Wellington, Route d'Agincourt or Route Blitzkrieg?'

'None of the Castellane waiters could give a bag of monkey's nuts that we were leaving.'

Alastair looked at the weeds on the track, at the broken signal and at the faded adverts on the platform for Brylcream and trilby hats, then dumped his things, put a colander on his head and walked onto the track, pretending to surf the rails.

'How long can I stay here?' he asked.

'About four hours.'

'When does the train come, then?'

'In about three.'

'One thing I learned that day was that Budapest was formed from two communities situated on either side of the river Danube: one called Buda, the other called Pest. (See, this book isn't just puerile, opinionated profanity – it's also educational, albeit in minuscule amounts.)'

'Praha Bubny was far and away the biggest rail-related dump I ever had the misfortune to set eyes upon. It was made from drab concrete which had become stained by the acid rain of the preceding years and by the sooty excrescence of the exhausts of the Ladas and Trabants which littered the city.'

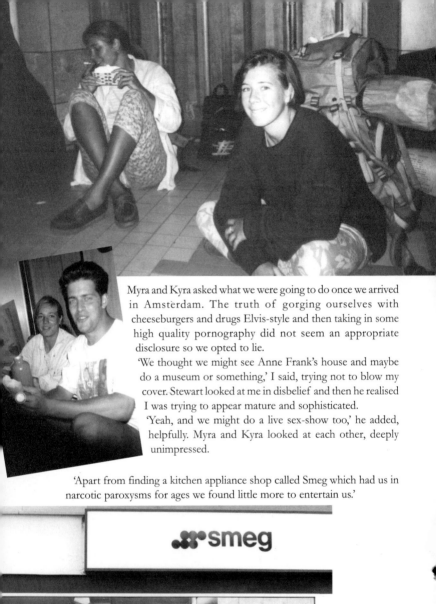

Myra and Kyra asked what we were going to do once we arrived in Amsterdam. The truth of gorging ourselves with cheeseburgers and drugs Elvis-style and then taking in some high quality pornography did not seem an appropriate disclosure so we opted to lie.

'We thought we might see Anne Frank's house and maybe do a museum or something,' I said, trying not to blow my cover. Stewart looked at me in disbelief and then he realised I was trying to appear mature and sophisticated.

'Yeah, and we might do a live sex-show too,' he added, helpfully. Myra and Kyra looked at each other, deeply unimpressed.

'Apart from finding a kitchen appliance shop called Smeg which had us in narcotic paroxysms for ages we found little more to entertain us.'

Do I win £5?

'Inter-Railers eager to sample the delights of Europe's premier porn and narcotic centre.'

'I stood steady now, guitar slung over my shoulder, milkshake in hand, while the others took a photo of me in front of a shop window full of vibrators.'

'By the time the border guards joined the train, we were happily unconscious in our sleeping bags, with only a larger than average dog-end on the floor remaining as evidence.'

'Are my nads showing through my trousers?' asked Alastair, pointing to the rip in his Indian hippie trousers through which one of his testicles was trying to see something of the world. 'Nah. Barely,' I said, sitting down on a bench adjacent to a decorative fountain, the centre piece of the little park. 'It's the trousers that cause the most offence, anyway.'

'Like washerwomen on the banks of the Ganges we stripped off our tops and scrubbed away at our clothes on the smooth rocks. Except Indian washerwomen probably didn't strip off. And we weren't on the banks of the Ganges.'

Before I could see the expression of indifference on her face, however, she exhaled again and completely vanished from view, during which there was so much confusion as I attempted blindly to kiss her goodbye that she dropped her cigarette onto her shoe.

'*Merde!*' she exclaimed, trying to rescue her foot and her fag.

Across the street I spied her primordial chums playing pinball at one of the town's rougher bars. It seemed wise to depart from the scene before the valves in their brains warmed up sufficiently to form a complete circuit, so we left Eva smouldering and returned to the tent. The main entrance to the campsite had to be avoided, of course, so we partially destroyed the wire fence close to our pitch by bending it right back, tearing our trousers as we clambered over.

– THE CITROËN POUBELLE –

STEWART

The bus that ran between Castellane and Digne every day resembled a giant mutilated bumper car. The driver, a stubbly peasant with a tobacco-stained goat on his lap, was barely visible through the dead flies on the windscreen and the occasional puff of smoke that leaked from his mouth. He was an elderly man, prone to playing *pétanque*, drinking Pastis and fulfilling any other Provençal cliché you could think of.

He was also an irritating masochist. Every morning he was up before sunrise, brushing the droppings out of the bus to make room for fresh ones and searching fruitlessly for his long-lost, thick spectacles. After a full mechanical check of his vehicle, to make sure it was still sufficiently unroadworthy, he would then drive it into the town centre. All this would take place before seven in the morning, at which point he would depart. This made us mad. It was an impossible time to aim for if you had a social life in the evenings. It wasn't healthy to be up that early. The cocks weren't crowing yet. Ours weren't even awake.

I don't know how it happened, but we missed the bus. We were disappointed, in the same way that someone who had failed to procure a ticket for the Titanic would have felt. There was now no way of getting to Digne, the nearest mainline station, without either buying a French 'car' or hitching a lift in someone else's. Buying a car for a twenty mile journey seemed a tad extravagant, so although hitching meant standing in the sun by the side of the road, there was no alternative. To avoid dehydration we decided to hitch from the road adjacent to the supermarket so that we could maintain a supply of chilled chocolate flavoured Yop, except during the four or five hours when it closed for lunch.

According to the cheap timepiece that covered the only unburnt part of my arm, we were now just a couple of Yops away from lunchtime. We had been roasting our thumbs for two hours. Our faces were covered with sticky chocolate Yop, to which some of the roadside dust and grime had quickly attached itself. Our shoes had filled with sweat until they leaked over the sides.

Anyone looking at the ground beneath my feet would have assumed I had wet myself.

'*Qu'est-ce que t'as fais, Stewart?*' I heard. I turned round to see Eva pointing at the puddle around my shoes. It was some time since we had said goodbye to everyone and I had already left Castellane mentally, if not physically, so it was odd to see a familiar face.

'He's pissed himself,' explained Alastair.

'*Trop de Yop.*'

'*Tu dis que des conneries,*' Eva decided. She looked tired after a hard morning's shoplifting in the supermarket, but at least she wasn't sweaty like us. The air conditioning system was one thing she hadn't yet stolen from her employers.

It later turned out that the combined efforts of all the check-out girls had twice led to the supermarket losing so much money that it had to be sold to rival companies, most recently to Casino. The girls' activities were in part due to laziness – zapping the bar codes on every item that came their way was a particularly unwelcome source of tedium – and in part due to philanthropy towards their hard-up friends. We had found it difficult paying for things even when we wanted to. They would just whisper *'Vite! Vite!'* and charge us for only the cheapest item in our shopping trolley. The excitement of our involvement in these major crimes was heightened by the sexual element: these were all lovely young ladies with whom there could have been no greater pleasure than to have shared a police cell.

It was the start of Eva's lunch chasm, and she had some interesting news for us.

'Tu vois l'homme avec le chapeau?' she asked, pointing to a doddery zombie in a seaside hat. He was walking painfully towards something between two parked cars, while fishing around in his pockets. He put a small piece of metal plucked from his trousers into the large piece of metal between two parked cars, and eased his frame into it. He vanished from sight.

'Why's he got a tin shack in this car park?' I asked. Eva tilted her head quizzically.

'Pourquoi il a un shag *dans ce parking? C'est ça tu m'as dis?'* she asked, thinking we were using some of the limited English vocabulary that was familiar to her.

The tin shack started rumbling and vibrating, then began very slowly to move.

'Is it a sort of Citroën?' asked Alastair.

'Yes, it's the Citroën *Poubelle*. A design classic,' I replied.

'Il va à Digne. Maintenant. Allez – vite!' shouted Eva.

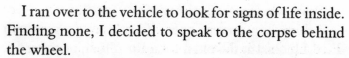

I ran over to the vehicle to look for signs of life inside. Finding none, I decided to speak to the corpse behind the wheel.

'*Monsieur? Nous faisons de l'autostop à Digne. Une fille qui travail dans le supermarché a dit que vous allez à Digne maintenant.*'

The car was still moving slowly forward, but I matched its pace without difficulty. The driver's head was slumped disconcertingly to one side, which made me feel that perhaps I was talking to myself, but eventually some air came rasping from his lungs and managed to form a word.

'*Eva?*' he asked, as if it were his dying word.

'*Oui, monsieur. C'est Eva.*'

The mention of Eva seemed to have a profound effect upon the man. He managed to lift his head and turn it towards me. He even stopped the car in order to deliver his next comment.

'*Elle est jolie, non? Très belles seins.*'

Alastair had by now joined me, carrying all the luggage. Geoff Capes couldn't have gone much further in the midday sun with two rucksacks and two guitars, and Alastair was utterly cream crackered.

'What's the verdict? Will he give us a lift?' he panted.

'I'm not sure,' I replied. 'All he's said is that Eva's got nice tits.'

'Shall we take that to mean yes?'

'I'll try again: *Monsieur – c'est vrai, ses seins sont très belles. Nous allons à Digne ensemble, alors?*'

'*Vous avez fait le jeu avec elle?*' he asked, with a feeble wink.

'What was that?' asked Alastair.

'I think he wants to know if I've played chess with Eva.' I looked at the old man again. '*Digne, monsieur?*'

'*Ouai, ouai,*' he replied, in his thickest Provençal drawl.

I lifted the piece of corrugated iron that seemed to cover the rear portion of the vehicle and dropped my rucksack onto the straw inside, holding it open while Alastair added his rucksack and the guits. As mobile dustbins went, this one was quite capacious.

I wanted to say goodbye to Eva, to thank her for procuring this lift for us, but she was already on her way to the tobacconists to steal some cigarettes.

Inside the *poubelle* was a lack of switches, dials and any recognisable form of vehicular control. It seemed to have been designed just after the war when there had been severe rationing of brain cells. If there was a speedometer, it was hidden in a recess behind a pile of tobacco. Someone had added a piece of cheesewire alongside the front passenger seat to serve as a seatbelt. I chose not to wear it.

The old man seemed to like having company. It brought him to life in much the same way as when he thought about Eva's *seins*.

Unfortunately, his renewed zest manifested itself in his style of driving. Once out of the car park and onto the Digne road, he drove like any other Frenchman in an underpowered and unroadworthy car, maniacally overtaking ahead of blind bends and achieving Formula One performance from a 2hp engine. He seemed to know the road fairly well because he barely put all four wheels on the ground at once.

It seemed polite to make small talk with the driver: to ask him if he lived in Digne; whether he had ever received driving lessons; and what job he used to do when he was alive. I was in the process of translating such phrases in my head when he spoke to us, turning his head away from the bendy mountain road to face us as he did so.

'*Voulez-vous voir les cascades?*' he asked, first once, then several times until I was able to understand him.

Of course we didn't. We just wanted to get to Digne, to catch a train, to get away from this madman. The last thing we wanted to do was to stop along the route and look at some boring waterfalls.

'*Oui,*' I replied, Britishly.

'*D'accord.*'

Our chauffeur began a long and incomprehensible monologue encompassing, as far as I could make out, waterfalls, grapes and Eva's tits. I nodded convincingly, trying to avoid eye contact in order to persuade him to look at the road occasionally. We overtook caravans and cyclists, pedestrians and police cars on a road surrounded by rugged mountain terrain and occasional medieval villages. For some time there had been a canyon alongside the road, gradually dropping deeper into oblivion as we gained height. I considered pointing out the presence of this canyon to the driver as I considered that it warranted a slightly less incautious approach to driving than he appeared to be taking, but he was already stopping before I could work out how to say 'slow down you crazy bastard' in French.

We pulled into one of those lay-bys that are the by-product of French road-straightening schemes. France is governed by people who live in the north of the country, where there are no hills and consequently no bends in the roads. These people experience enormous difficulty when they travel south all at once on 14th July each year with their caravans and suddenly have to remember how to use their steering wheels. Their solution is an on-going programme of road-straightening, ironing out the curves until they will one day be able to drive from Paris to Cannes without removing their steering locks.

The old bend had become littered over the years with dust, gravel and the faeces of French tourists. The 'new bit', by contrast, was pure, gleaming concrete, all the way down to the rocky river below us. Alastair and I ran over to the bright silver crash barrier, leaning over to look down at the waterfalls. The barrier was hot to touch, and my hands danced around on its surface trying not to burn. The driver remained in the car.

'Should we pretend to take a photo?' I suggested, not wanting to offend our driver. With the sun directly overhead the river was sparkling over the rocks, crashing down from one level to another about ten feet below, looking like Perrier being poured into a rocky canyon. Or something.

'Hey, what's he doing?' shouted Alastair, looking back at the car.

I could hear the panels vibrating as he fired up the engine, and as I turned round I saw the car start to move.

Everything we owned was in his boot.

The last time I had felt so badly conned was when I entered a peep show that boasted '£1 only – no extras' outside and where, despite starting off with £10 in my pocket, I had run out of money before I'd even managed a peep. This old bastard had tricked us into leaving all our gear in his boot, and now he was driving off, leaving us miles from civilisation, miles from a McDonald's even, with no money, no passport, and no intellectual credibility. How could I have been so stupid?

He was moving slowly at this stage, as if trying to sneak away without us noticing. Dust was billowing from behind the car as it edged closer to the concrete road, on the far side of which we stood.

Motivated entirely by anger, I ran across the road and threw myself onto the bonnet, scowling through the windscreen at the driver. As I did so, however, I could already sense that the car had not been accelerating. Indeed, it had been slowing down before I had even started running. There was no other traffic for him to give way to, and the horrifying thought entered my head that I may have been a little hasty in my judgement. In retrospect, it seemed likely that he was just moving the car closer to us. What he thought of my antics I don't know, but once back inside the car again no words were spoken during the rest of the journey. I sat in embarrassed silence, contemplating the old man, wondering whether someone of that age would even have it in them to commit theft. He didn't have it in him to commit many other sins, that was certain.

*

At the station was a large, oval shaped roundabout for dropping off people. It sloped steeply up hill towards the ticket office, so our considerate driver let us out at

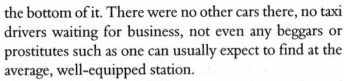

the bottom of it. There were no other cars there, no taxi drivers waiting for business, not even any beggars or prostitutes such as one can usually expect to find at the average, well-equipped station.

Once at the top of the hill we were hot, sticky and miserable. I badly needed a cold drink but the only dispensing machine served condoms.

Alastair called me away from the machine that had eaten my money and refused to give me any *preservatifs* in order to look at the timetable next to the ticket office. He was concerned that no trains appeared to run from Digne that day.

'Impossible,' I bluffed. 'This is a mainline station. I'll ask the fascist when the next one is due.'

The tiny window into the world of ticket-issuing was a little low for me, making me stoop as I spoke to the fascist inside.

'*Un train?*' asked the ticket fascist, bemused. '*Le prochain train?*' he continued. He turned to his colleague to seek an explanation for this bizarre phrase, but their combined years of service at this railway station had not prepared them for such a difficult question.

'*Vous allez-où, monsieur?*' asked his colleague.

'Paris,' I replied.

'*Paris?*' he exclaimed, as if I had said Jupiter. '*En train?*'

I was too confused by his attitude to bother correcting his grammar. Until today I had been fairly certain that Paris possessed a railway station. I had even believed that its first railways had been built by the British, which is why they ran on the left, but now I was not so sure about anything.

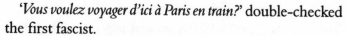

'*Vous voulez voyager d'ici à Paris en train?*' double-checked the first fascist.

'*D'ici?*' emphasised the other.

I nodded, without anticipation that my affirmation would lead ultimately to any information other than that I shouldn't be contemplating catching a train from here to France's most easy-to-get-to destination.

'*Attendez,*' growled the first one, then went to find the station's copy of the 1938 railway timetable.

'*Paris – impossible. Veynes, oui. Puis changez.*'

Why was it vain of me to want to go to Paris? I looked at the faded ink on the bloodstained page and saw that there was indeed a train leaving from this station today. It was going to that well known and useful destination, Veynes, which was just about the only place I could see in the book at all. I mentioned to Alastair that there appeared to be a minor chance of escaping that afternoon and perhaps even of getting to Gare du Nord in time for our rendezvous with Paul tomorrow. He looked at the weeds on the track, at the broken signal and at the faded adverts on the platform for Brylcream and trilby hats, then dumped his things, put a colander on his head and walked onto the track, pretending to surf the rails.

'How long can I stay here?' he asked.

'About four hours.'

'When does the train come, then?'

'In about three.'

PAUL

Sunday saw me doing very little. My parents' labour force, consisting of all those who had stayed the night,

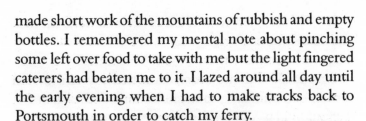

made short work of the mountains of rubbish and empty bottles. I remembered my mental note about pinching some left over food to take with me but the light fingered caterers had beaten me to it. I lazed around all day until the early evening when I had to make tracks back to Portsmouth in order to catch my ferry.

There was a short queue ahead of me at the ticket desk once I reached the ferry terminal. At the time I thought nothing of it, sparked a cigarette and began to worry about the chances of actually meeting up with the other two the next day in Paris. The queue edged slowly closer to the desk and, just as I concluded that I had a fifty-fifty chance of making a successful rendezvous with the others, it was my turn at the counter.

'A single to Le Havre please. One foot passenger with an Inter-Rail discount.'

'I'm sorry, sir, the sailing is fully booked. You can be put on the waitlist if you like?'

I simply thought that the ticket fascist had misunderstood me.

'No, it's just me. I don't have a car. I'm a foot passenger.'

'I appreciate that, sir, but we are fully booked and we are only licensed to carry so many people.'

I dejectedly accepted my position as penultimate bloke on the waitlist, and shuffled over to a bench to wait for someone who had pre-booked not to show up. The man who had been standing behind me came and joined me on the bench.

'Don't worry, my friend. We will get on the boat.'

My fellow waitlister was a Frenchman called Max. Apparently he often encountered this 'ferry is full' hiccup but was confident that we would ultimately get our tickets. If I'd thought about it rationally then I would almost certainly have agreed with him. The chances of every single pre-booked passenger turning up on time from all over the country were indeed slim, but my mind could only imagine worst case scenarios. Those people ahead of me in the waitlist queue were being paged one or two at a time until there was just Max and me left. There were six minutes until the ferry sailed and I feared the worst.

The seconds dragged on.

Finally, the ticket clerk beckoned to me.

'See you soon I hope, Max,' I said as I jogged for the door. At the end of a passage that led from the door was a shuttle bus with no one on it except for the driver. A little extravagant, I thought. I could have walked it, if necessary. The bus sat motionless with the engine running. Three minutes until the ship was due to leave. The driver engaged first gear, made about twenty feet's worth of progress and then came to an abrupt halt. The doors opened and in came Max looking completely unfazed.

We got talking and he told me he was the bar manager for a very famous hotel on Park Lane and that he was going to visit his sister in Le Havre. Once on board the boat he insisted on buying me a bottle of Grolsch as we nattered away as if we were the best of friends. Another Grolsch followed and then another two at once as the

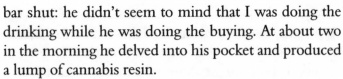

bar shut: he didn't seem to mind that I was doing the drinking while he was doing the buying. At about two in the morning he delved into his pocket and produced a lump of cannabis resin.

'Are you insane?' I asked, dumbfounded that he should have carried drugs through customs.

'Is not a problem. Anyway, ze drugs are leaving England so why should anyone care?'

He had a point, though I'm not sure that it would have stood up in court. He proceeded to roll a reefer, indifferent to the closed circuit television system which was showing coverage of his skinning-up operation on a black and white monitor behind the now shuttered bar. I looked around with trepidation. The bar was full of shellsuit-attired plebs snoozing on the bar seats next to their piles of duty free. It was a very strange feeling but I joined Mad Max in smoking a spliff before I skulked off to the heavily padded children's play area to pass out.

★

I woke up much sooner than I would have liked. I looked out of the port window to see the quayside running parallel to the ship. A few children were looking at me in disappointment as their parents glowered down at me. I muttered something about 6 a.m. being far too early to be playing anyway and returned to the bar where Max was readying himself for disembarkation.

'Where do you go now?' he asked.

'The train station. I'll have to hurry – I've only got twenty minutes.'

'I'll give you a lift if it will help.'

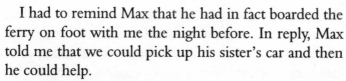

I had to remind Max that he had in fact boarded the ferry on foot with me the night before. In reply, Max told me that we could pick up his sister's car and then he could help.

Luckily we cleared customs without incident and we set off at a half-jog towards the centre of Le Havre. Arriving at a drab, dirty building with cracked masonry Max started rapping on the shutters of a ground floor window.

'Agnes! Agnes! Agnes! Lêves-toi! Agnes!'

Someone in a building on the other side of the street opened their window and shouted at him to shut his gob. Agnes appeared in the window looking less than pleased to have been awoken in this way. Max procured the keys from her and we set off at a typically French speed towards the station. I was mightily impressed by Max: he was one of the few European men I met while abroad who had been hospitable for no other reason than honest friendship. He set me down at the station, performed a brisk U-turn in the road, shouted *'Salut!'* and he was gone.

I had a very brief wait for my train, which I then boarded and fell immediately into a deep sleep from which I did not awaken until Paris.

STEWART

I felt like a portion of French fries when I arrived in Paris: hot, greasy and with a sweaty packet. I was also hungry, but before I could take in any nourishment there was the overriding necessity of downloading my insides into a suitable receptacle in order to make room for the

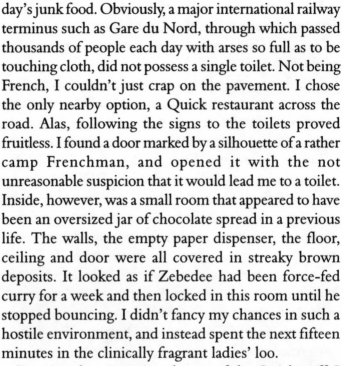

day's junk food. Obviously, a major international railway terminus such as Gare du Nord, through which passed thousands of people each day with arses so full as to be touching cloth, did not possess a single toilet. Not being French, I couldn't just crap on the pavement. I chose the only nearby option, a Quick restaurant across the road. Alas, following the signs to the toilets proved fruitless. I found a door marked by a silhouette of a rather camp Frenchman, and opened it with the not unreasonable suspicion that it would lead me to a toilet. Inside, however, was a small room that appeared to have been an oversized jar of chocolate spread in a previous life. The walls, the empty paper dispenser, the floor, ceiling and door were all covered in streaky brown deposits. It looked as if Zebedee had been force-fed curry for a week and then locked in this room until he stopped bouncing. I didn't fancy my chances in such a hostile environment, and instead spent the next fifteen minutes in the clinically fragrant ladies' loo.

Ignoring the aggressive glances of the Quick staff, I returned to base without purchasing an armful of burgers and chips. There was no better way I could think of to protest about the lack of hygiene in the restaurant. Other than actually protesting about it.

Paul arrived on time, but there was something odd about him that we couldn't quite place. It wasn't that he had become a brother-in-law since we had last seen him, or that he had drunk too much at the wedding. He sensed our disquiet, and decided to own up.

'My mum made me have a bath. You know, for the wedding. It'll wear off soon.'

PAUL

The interrogation I received at the hands of the others was not what I needed after such a narcotic-filled evening with Max, and I was able to persuade Stewart and Alastair that I needed to sleep. The others chattered to each other as I traipsed silently behind them, looking for a place to doss. Paris, like all other large cities, is short on dossing space. While a penthouse might set you back a cool million and a posh gaff in Le Vesinet might cost half that, even the budget accommodation which we sought was in short supply in this fine city. Every promising-looking place, on closer inspection, revealed either a tramp already in residence or a large amount of excrescence. Or both.

I was the most tired I have ever been and I would have been happy to fall asleep on my feet in a handy phone box, but even these were all fully occupied by fat Americans phoning home to report how they had 'done' France and were going to 'do' Italy on Wednesday and then Greece on Thursday. After an eternal perambulation, which as far I was concerned may as well have been the Israelites' exodus from Egypt, we passed the highly posh Galleries Lafayette, a pointy obelisk like Cleopatra's needle and found a park which, between the piles of dog shite and Japanese tourists, was a space large enough for three Inter-Railers, three rucksacks and three guitars. Instantly I fell asleep. Occasionally we would wake with a start as groups of inquisitive tourists and locals alike would loom over us seeing if we were dead or sufficiently asleep to make a good target for robbery.

147

Eventually, at about three in the afternoon, we had reached a point where we felt sufficiently refreshed to tackle drinking some beer. We wandered from place to place finding a reason not to enter at every venue. Too posh, too scabby, too full, too empty – must be something dodgy about it, too dark, and so on. Despite our protestations we finally settled at a bar called Bar Notre Dame. Unsurprisingly it was in the shadow of Notre Dame cathedral and therefore the most expensive place outside of the Tour d'Argent. We piled our crap as inconspicuously as possible behind some unused chairs and started preparing ourselves for the impending shock of being exposed to the prices on the menu. Finding the price for a large beer to be a snip at a mere five pounds, Alastair and I ordered a large one each while Stewart had a rum and coke.

'Girl!' shouted Alastair and I in unison as Stewart's poncey refreshment arrived. Stewart was spared further taunting by the arrival of a sight more pitiful than his taste in alcohol. On one of the anti-ramraid bollards that ran in a bizarre line across the filthy frontage of Paris' most famous but least impressive ecclesiastical edifice was an 'Automat': Alastair's absolute favourite form of street entertainer. Except pan-pipe buskers, obviously. After the sort of preparation you normally see Olympic athletes subjecting themselves to, the pointless clown attracted the attention of as many passers-by as possible. Then he began moving in the kind of exaggerated, mechanical movements one would normally expect to see from Stewart when he is playing drums. After a minute or so of movement he would stand stock-still in whatever pose he deemed appropriate until someone came forward to put some money in his hat. This, of course, made the audience more resolute to make him retain his static poses for as long as possible: the more uncomfortable that pose looked, the better.

I thought what he was doing, though not very amusing in itself, took an impressive amount of composure and dexterity.

Alastair just thought the Automat was a twat.

Once the Automat got his money he would start moving again for a few moments and then stop. This was the extent of his act and people soon became bored of it. Dull though the Automat undoubtedly was, stupid he was not. He had chosen such a central and busy part of Paris that no sooner had one set of bored punters drifted off but another load came to replace the shortfall. He looked to be earning a tidy sum and we resentfully turned our backs on him and started making plans for our escape to Amsterdam later that evening. The conversation was daintily gracing the topics of pornography and controlled substances when we became aware of something attention-grabbing happening behind us. Obviously nothing to do with the Automat, we thought. In fact we were wrong. Unwittingly and certainly unconsentingly, the sad excuse for entertainment was putting in a finale that no one had foreseen. No one, that is, apart from the woman who was running towards us with his hat full of small change.

'*Salope!*' cried the hapless idiot whose entire earnings were now heading at a rate of knots into the backstreets. '*Putain!*' he added in case it made a difference.

We laughed at him as he tore past us and we wondered what the chances were of his recovering all his other possessions, which were abandoned at the foot of his erstwhile perch, once he returned. Cyber-Pierrot's fate seemed to have breathed a new life and purpose into the clown-hating Alastair who ordered another round of drinks to celebrate the mime's misfortune. Once we considered the scenario of the same thing happening to us it wasn't so funny, at least not for the few seconds that we considered the situation for, after which we returned to the more enjoyable pastime of *schadenfreude*.

We knew what to expect at Gare du Nord, though we were pointlessly optimistic that the station would not be awash with Inter-Railers eager to sample the delights of Europe's premier porn and narcotic centre. Of course, when we did arrive the platform was, as predicted, a seething mass of college students gobbing-off to each other about how to skin up a cone that Marley himself would have been proud of while hoping that they would be able to learn the basics of how to roll dried vegetation in paper before they were expected to demonstrate these skills. We snobbishly ignored them, such was our status as seasoned Inter-Railers, and squeezed our crap through the throng to an unused patch of platform at the far end of the station.

STEWART

The entire population of Paris was crammed into Gare du Nord upon our return, and when the platform for the 23:17 Amsterdam train was announced it became clear that they were all coming with us. All our hard-earned knowledge of Inter-Rail tactics was going to be needed if we were to secure a compartment for ourselves, but considering we had already written a book on such a topic we didn't expect this to be a problem.

Phase one went according to plan: we spread ourselves along the platform at intervals of ten feet in order to triple the chances of one of us being close to a door when the train stopped. Paul struck it lucky, once he had shoved a few irritating kids out of the way, and entered the carriage before anyone else. Following Inter-Rail procedure to the letter, he then instigated phase two. For this phase he sprinted to a compartment towards the centre of the carriage, dived inside, spread his luggage all over the seats, took off his shoes, and waited for the rancid fumes from his feet to fill the air. But there was a flaw in this part of the plan, as I noticed when I caught up with him and discovered to my horror that five unwelcome sweaty foreigners had joined him in our compartment. Paul's feet had failed utterly as a deterrent – the bath he had been forced to take had killed off entire colonies of the microbes upon which we so heavily relied in the cause of Inter-Railing. Every other compartment was now full, so I was forced, despite all my professed prowess as an Inter-Rail tactician, to sleep in the narrow, dusty corridor, getting kicked by people when they went to the loo, and getting dripped on when they came back.

As the night wore on, the kicks became less frequent and my periods of sleep grew longer and deeper. The person next to me in the narrow corridor, whose feet were pressing against my head due to the lack of space, was snoring like a bronchial elephant, but the sound

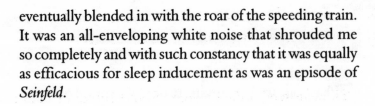

eventually blended in with the roar of the speeding train. It was an all-enveloping white noise that shrouded me so completely and with such constancy that it was equally as efficacious for sleep inducement as was an episode of *Seinfeld*.

– THE SINGLE GENTLEMAN'S ENTERTAINMENT EMPORIUM –

STEWART

'Hey, misters!' called a voice from behind a bank of telephones as we left the platform at Amsterdam Centraal. You don't arrive in Amsterdam expecting to be greeted by nuns offering garlands of flowers or brass bands welcoming you with renditions of *The Floral Dance*, so we were prepared for the inevitable barrage of unsavoury offers from dubious characters lurking in every shadow. I turned to face the living embodiment of Shaggy from *Scooby-Doo* — a spaced-out hippie with straggly hair, bristles and torn denim clothes. For someone who appeared to be little more than litter (litter is just below Inter-Railers in the hierarchy of lowlife), he turned out to be a versatile agent of adult entertainment, offering to fulfil any illegal, perverse, sick or just immoral ambitions that we may wish to achieve during our short stay in the city. Much of what he had to offer was wrapped in foil packages in the stained inside pocket of his jacket, but other unappealing options were available elsewhere about his person.

We didn't look back until we had run up a flight of stairs where we blended into the melée of people in the main station concourse. Further escapes from excessively helpful natives would be easier without the encumbrances of our luggage, it was decided, so we dumped the rucksacks in a locker and went out into the world to look for breakfast.

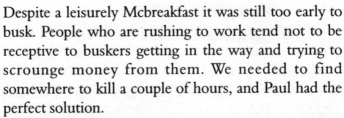

Despite a leisurely Mcbreakfast it was still too early to busk. People who are rushing to work tend not to be receptive to buskers getting in the way and trying to scrounge money from them. We needed to find somewhere to kill a couple of hours, and Paul had the perfect solution.

'It's just around the corner, if I remember correctly. I went there last year with Olly.'

'What exactly is it?' I asked.

'A kind of entertainment centre, specialising in the recorded televisual arts, just for gentlemen,' he explained.

'Sounds very wholesome,' said Alastair.

'Oh, indeed. Very wholesome, and very discreet.'

'Why would discretion be important?' I wanted to know.

'It would be indiscreet of me to tell you,' evaded Paul.

We turned the corner, heading away from the busier roads into a quiet, respectable-looking street. There were no obvious sources of entertainment for gentlemen in the street at all, not even any shops except for an ordinary video shop on the corner.

As we entered the video shop I checked to see if any of us had remembered to bring a video player on the trip, but none of us had. Paul was saying nothing, but I assumed he intended to ask the shop proprietor for directions. The little Dutchman had just finished opening up and was setting his till when Paul approached him.

'Three, please,' said Paul, bizarrely, handing over a large proportion of our precious cash.

'What are you doing?' asked Alastair.

'How are we supposed to watch a video?' I wanted to know.

'It's a kind of mini-cinema. You choose what you want to watch, and then go to a private booth to watch it. You don't need to take the film home,' he explained.

What an excellent concept, I thought. Perfect for groups of friends who can't agree on a choice of film. Perfect also for a tourist looking for a little light entertainment to break the monotony of Amsterdam sightseeing, shopping, and cannabis smoking.

I took a closer look at the choice of Dutch videos spread across the shelves around me. Despite the shop's conservative façade, every title on display inside was of an adult leaning. It seemed rather early in the morning to be leaning in such a direction, but Paul was already virtually bent double, reading the backs of some of the boxes.

'I've only paid for half-hour films. Make sure you choose the right length,' said Paul.

'Are you sure we've got a booth each?' I checked.

'Just give the nice man your video, and he'll give you a number. Go upstairs to the door with your number on, and your video will be playing inside. It's simple.'

How, I wondered, was I going to be able to give this man – a total stranger — my video choice and look him in the eye when he gave me my booth number? How was it possible to do that without him thinking I was a sad pervert?

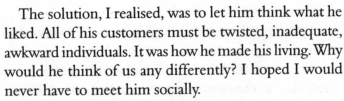

The solution, I realised, was to let him think what he liked. All of his customers must be twisted, inadequate, awkward individuals. It was how he made his living. Why would he think of us any differently? I hoped I would never have to meet him socially.

I made my selection quickly, not wanting to appear to be a choosy connoisseur of films that were so low budget they couldn't even afford clothes for the actors. The man retained the video and gave me a key labelled '2'. Film buffs 1 and 3 led the way upstairs to a dark, windowless corridor lined with numbered doors.

'See you later,' I said to them, as we each entered our separate offices for the start of the day's work.

Inside, I hung my guitar on the handy peg and sat down. The room was no larger than a toilet cubicle, dimly lit from a filtered fluorescent strip light. A television screen flickered in front of me, showing the copyright warning at the start of the film – 'This film is a pirate copy, and breaks all possible copyright legislation' – it was in Dutch, of course, but that was what it probably meant. Immediately below the screen was a small sink, and below that was a swing-bin. The final embellishment to this self-contained pleasure palace was a toilet roll on a wall-mounted dispenser.

I managed a quick pee into the sink, then sat back before the show started. I could sense faint vibrations coming through the walls around me, sending perceptible ripples through the dangling tissues and making the drips from the tap fall off-centre. Major roadworks must have been set up outside in the last five

156

minutes. Or possibly a large consignment of Edam had been accidentally dropped whilst being delivered to a local cheese shop. Despite what was happening on the television in front of me – it seemed to be a trailer for an adult movie that was being shown before my chosen Disney cartoon – I started thinking about cheese delivery men and whether they would need to wear steel toe capped boots. It was possible that they delivered their enormous cheeses by rolling them along the ground, safely wrapped in a protective layer of red wax. But the cheese would need to be wrapped in wax, too. Ooh, I thought, suddenly distracted from my cheese theories, they appeared to have lost their clothes between the kitchen and the living room. The lady of the house and her lady visitor seemed to want to get to know each other quite well. They were managing to do so without even speaking. I expected that Mr Video downstairs would eventually realise his mistake and change the tape for me, but there seemed no point in complaining.

Half an hour later, we met, awkwardly, once again in the corridor, and squeezed with our guitars down the stairs, past a jolly, uninhibited Dutchman trotting upstairs for his morning wank.

'Hoi!' he said to us, grinning widely. He checked the number on his key, then vanished into a cubicle.

It was going to be a strange day.

★

With so much of our cash spent on strangling our snakes, there was barely enough with which to help the economies of third world countries by buying their

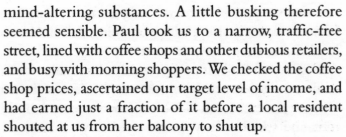
mind-altering substances. A little busking therefore seemed sensible. Paul took us to a narrow, traffic-free street, lined with coffee shops and other dubious retailers, and busy with morning shoppers. We checked the coffee shop prices, ascertained our target level of income, and had earned just a fraction of it before a local resident shouted at us from her balcony to shut up.

'Dey are barshtards,' offered a sympathetic shopper as she put some coins into my hand. 'Why don't you ignore her?'

'Because we are guests in this country,' I said.

The woman began to walk away.

'Because we are lazy, we hate busking and we want to spend your money on some drugs,' added Paul.

The woman turned round and gave him a thumbs-up. People's attitudes in this country never ceased to amaze me. Busking in England, I was once offered money by an old lady on the specific and patronising condition that I didn't spend it on alcohol or drugs. Did she get the same kind of talking to from the Post Office clerk when she collected her pension? 'Here's your pension, Mrs Snodgrass. Now, don't you go blowing it all on young male prostitutes, Stout and Sanatogen.' I doubt it. It wasn't difficult for me to comply – she hadn't given me enough.

We packed up and entered the nearest coffee shop. After a quick drink, we purchased a few goodies to take away. I chose a little piece of cake for elevenses. We drifted along the street away from the coffee shop, through to a busy square which would have been a much more lucrative site had we been that way inclined, and then followed some canals until we arrived at a footbridge overlooking a floating police station.

Alastair and Paul sat on the fence and mellowed out, sharing the goodies they had just bought. For me, it was time for elevenses. It took a bite of my cake, reluctantly at first because I had no idea how good it would taste. It was a cross between a flapjack and a spongecake, and, despite the questionable ingredients, it was delicious. The others were laughing and joking now, giggling about the police station on the canal and discussing to which country we would shortly have to flee. They were in buoyant mood, but I still had a craving for more of that delicious cake, the first one having made little impression on me. 'Are you sure you want another?' asked Paul. 'I think you should wait a bit longer. Let the first one get down.'

'I'll be fine,' I bluffed. 'You two wait here. I won't be long.' Leaving my guitar with them, I trotted off, blissfully unencumbered by anything dull like luggage or common sense. Instantly I was lost. All the canals looked the same, all the houses looked like Anne Frank's, and I couldn't navigate by the sun because it was cloudy and anyway I didn't know how to. It didn't matter though. There were coffee shops all over Amsterdam. They all served the same things: coffee, cakes, goodies.

I turned down a sidestreet then took a path alongside a canal. A tourist barge chugged alongside me, matching my speed.

'On your right,' the commentator seemed to be saying, 'you can see Anne Frank's house. And there's another one. On your left, you can see a tourist, searching for coffee shops and brothels. Well, he's in luck, because we've almost come to our destination today, ladies and gentlemen, the red light district.'

The barge stopped. Next to it, across the canal from where I was walking, was a building with a shop window frontage displaying semi-naked oriental women. Outside stood a bouncer, who promptly welcomed a party of Japanese businessmen as they got off the barge.

There were similar 'shops' on my side of the canal, too. In each one, a grotesque lady would be seated on a leather chair behind a plate glass window, wearing nothing but a few wisps of lace and a G-string. Outside each one, a hefty gentleman would invite me to partake of their entertainment, at reasonable tourist rates. I politely declined them all, having already fully partaken that morning. Finally, I came to a coffee shop. It didn't look as friendly as the other one. The building was in a poor state of repair, the frontage was badly painted in a Rastafarian colour scheme, and the clientele looked like gangsters. They kept their machine guns out of sight as I stepped into a hushed silence. I spotted a cake tray containing a ropy piece of homemade cake that looked as if it had been left there all week. But it was cheap.

'*Een cake, als het U belieft,*' I said to the owner, hoping that I had pronounced it right and hadn't inadvertently called his mother a walrus.

The gangsters now ignored me. So did the owner.

'*Als het U belieft,*' I squeaked, trying to get his attention.

This time he turned his scarred face to me. Someone had once tried to extend his mouth across to his ear. They had very nearly succeeded. '*Een cake, als het U belieft.*'

The coffee shop owner lifted the Perspex lid from the cake tray.

It was at this point that I noticed how filthy his hands were. Never mind, I thought, he's got some tongs behind him. Which was where they stayed. He picked up the cake, his fingernails digging in so tight that it started to crumble at the edges, and plonked it on the painted wooden counter.

'*Dank U,*' I said, paying him. I grabbed the cake and made a hasty exit before anyone tried to shoot me.

Finding my way back past the brothels was fairly easy. Again, I had to refuse their kind offers with a polite shake of the head as I stuffed myself with the most bitter, blotchy and bodged cake I had eaten since the days of school dinners.

*

There must have been something slightly odd in that second cake. Perhaps I shouldn't have eaten it whilst walking so fast, but by the time I had located Paul and Alastair the ground seemed to have lost a little of its solidity. Something in my stomach not only disagreed with me, it was passionately arguing with me, telling me that I shouldn't have eaten a second cake. Nonsense, I told it. Digest it and shut up.

There was a small amount of activity on the police barge below us; blond moustached policemen walking on board at the end of their shifts and more blond moustached policemen getting off to replace them. I wondered what went on inside that floating Portakabin, but had no intention of finding out. We left the vicinity in a different direction from that which offered the opportunity of sex at a pimp's gunpoint with fat, diseased prostitutes. There was only enough cash left for a McDonald's.

The spongy pavement beneath my feet gave a spring to my step that wobbled my guitar into the paths of oncoming pedestrians. Weak shafts of light reflecting off windows from a dull, hazy sun made me screw up my eyes excessively. I was holding the guitar carefully now, with both hands: it felt lighter than a creamy beige, and softer than the weakest disciplinary measure. The others were talking, loudly and quickly. It wasn't great philosophy, for once, but the simple words went into my head as sounds and remained undecoded, floating around in search of connections, finding none, and buggering off again.

I didn't want to be run over by a big, yellow Dutch tram. I was certain of that. Trams didn't steer round you very well, and with the roads being somewhat rubbery and unsubstantial today, I took things very carefully when crossing a wide road to McDonald's.

But it was too early for lunch. Adjacent was a cinema, and we all needed to sit down having been walking incessantly for more than four minutes. Paul led the way inside, past all the movie souvenirs and spin-offs, straight to the ticket booth.

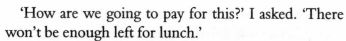

'How are we going to pay for this?' I asked. 'There won't be enough left for lunch.'

'Do you take credit cards?' asked Alastair.

'Certainly, sir,' replied the voice in the booth.

'Three then, please,' said Paul, who was getting good at it.

The cinema had two screens, one at either side of the top of the stairs. I bounced up them, holding on tight to the handrail in case there were any yellow trams around. It occurred to me that we didn't know what films were showing. We didn't even know if they were in Dutch or English. It didn't occur to me that there wouldn't be any trams on the stairs, though. Sad, really.

'This is the choice, then boys,' announced Paul. 'Screen One is offering *Toby and Tim's Tight Trousers*. Hmm. And Screen Two is offering *Virgin Chalet Girls*. Not for long, I suspect.'

We all bundled into Screen Two through the narrow doorway. The film had already started, and very few seats remained. Paul and I squeezed into the centre of a row, leaving Alastair and all the guitars to lie on the floor in front of everyone.

I sat back and looked at the ceiling. I looked at the other members of the audience whilst trying not to look at the audience's members.

Paul nudged me to look at the film, but he was too late. I passed out.

★

About an hour later I woke up. I was still seated, looking ahead at a big bright patch of light. My neck wouldn't move, but it didn't need to. I sat motionless, bombarded by a light that was full of moving shapes, curling around each other, twirling and chasing. It was like an action cartoon, a cat and mouse chase, a train coming out of a tunnel to run over the cat and a triumphant mouse returning to his cheesy hole in the wainscoting.

I soon realised that this wasn't a cartoon. The light slowly focused and the bizarre cat and mouse images metamorphosed into an energetically copulating couple, rolling in the crisp snow in front of majestic Swiss mountains. This was not usually the first thing I saw when I woke up. Paul was still next to me.

'Huh,' I said to him.

'Did you have a nice sleep, Poo?' he asked.

'Huh.'

I blinked hard and tried to instil some consciousness into my brain.

All around me strange Dutchmen and tourists were masturbating furiously beneath their summer raincoats. Probably. My arms wouldn't even move.

'Have you kept up with the plot?' asked Paul.

'Huh,' I said.

The chalet girl rolled down the snow to a second gentleman, who seemed to have been patiently waiting his turn. They looked terribly chilly. It made me shiver.

In the final few minutes of the film, I deduced the finer points of the plot: the chalet girls have quite of lot of sex with the chalet boys. Feeling thoroughly edified from coping with the complexities of that Plutarchian epic, I tried to stand up.

What's so great about standing up, anyway, I wondered? The chairs in this place were very comfortable. I sat back, letting the other gentlemen in the cinema leave first. They looked like a line of Daleks. I needed some time to reconnect my brain to the various parts of my body required for exiting the cinema. An attempt at moving my right leg resulted in a noticeable twitching of my left ear. Then I tried my left leg, which got my right ear flapping like a fish out of water (and glued to the side of my head so it wouldn't fall off). Aha, I thought. I tried flapping both ears, and promptly leapt to my feet. This was getting easy. Once I had finished re-wiring the vandalised telephone exchange in my head, I would be able to leave before the chalet girls came out for more Helvetican frolics.

As I followed Paul to the edge of our row of seats, I wanted to steady myself by placing my hand on an adjacent seat back, but had to make do with hearing myself say the word 'longjohns'. Alastair passed me my guitar, and I was ready.

'Longjohns,' I tried to say, but instead my hand went out to accept the proffered instrument, exactly as I had planned. As the near-normality of an Inter-Railer's reality returned, I wondered what body action I would have to do to say the word 'cheeseburger' when we dined next door?

Downstairs I could see that the souvenirs and film tie-ins I thought I had seen on the way in were no more than shelves of sundry masturbatory accessories: dildos, prurient magazines and books, and strange contraptions

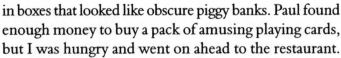

in boxes that looked like obscure piggy banks. Paul found enough money to buy a pack of amusing playing cards, but I was hungry and went on ahead to the restaurant.

We sat upstairs, hunched around two square, plastic-coated McTables. The place was filling quite rapidly as lunchtime got into full swing, so I put on my green tinted Lennon specs to hide the chaos in my eyes. Instead, I now looked like a hippie. Paul soon plonked a modest tray of burgers and drinks on the table.

'That was the last of the cash, lads. Enjoy the meal,' he said.

I received only a fraction of what I had asked him for, so I wanted to make the most of the one, small cheeseburger in front of me.

'Do you mind if I put some of those *herbes de Provence* in my burger? Spice it up a little?' I asked.

'You're crazy,' replied Paul, waving the little sachet in front of me as if he were trying to revive me with smelling salts. 'This is a public place. You're not up to it.'

'It's just a few herbs,' I objected. 'No one cares. This is Holland. They probably put them in the burgers anyway.'

I grabbed the sachet from him, opened up my burger, fished out the gherkin, and sprinkled a layer of dry, green, exotic herbs onto the meat. The others looked at me as if I had just pushed a nun out of a window (again). I was too busy chomping, pleased that my mouth was obeying instructions again.

The burger tasted as if I'd dropped it onto a recently mowed summer lawn and not bothered scraping off the grass. Or anything else which may have attached itself. I ate quickly, hoping the taste would soon dissolve from my tongue, washed down with a hearty milkshake.

'Is this table loose?' I asked, putting my drink down and sensing that the tabletop was no longer flat. No one was listening to me. 'Hey, watch your drinks – they'll fall off the edge.'

To everyone's annoyance, I picked up their drinks and moved them closer to the centre of the table.

'Uh-oh, it's tilting the other way now,' I exclaimed, horrified at the inferior construction of the building. I began to slide helplessly across my seat, pressing my feet into the floor in an effort to steady myself. The table started to sway even further: I was sure all of our drinks would end up dropping onto the floor. 'Watch yourselves,' I warned, as the others nonchalantly continued eating and chatting. If they weren't going to help me I would have to save the day by myself. I braced my feet against the subsiding floor, held my arms around the edges of the table so that no drinks would slide off it, and hung on grimly. Coping with Amsterdam's sudden and frightening instability was an ordeal that kept me occupied for the duration of our meal. I felt seasick. I wondered whether I would slide sideways and out of the window, or whether the place might flip over completely.

'What's up with Poo?' I heard Alastair ask.

'I think he needs a holiday,' said Paul.

They helped me up, and carried my guitar for me as we descended the stairs that had twisted and buckled to a steep and slippery angle. I dropped down the last few steps with only my arms to break my fall. It had been like an escape from a haunted house in a funfair, with walls moving, floors giving way, and strange ghoulish characters in the shadows. Rather like my student houses at university, too, only there was less McDonald's packaging littering the floor here in Amsterdam.

My first steps outside brought instant relief from my private disaster movie. It was as if Kirk Douglas had plucked me from the top of the towering inferno, lifted me to safety, and sorted out all the complicated insurance claim forms for me. What a hero. I stood steady now, guitar slung over my shoulder, milkshake in hand, while the others took a photo of me in front of a shop window full of vibrators.

*

We managed to stay out of trouble for most of the afternoon, which was quite an achievement considering the abundance of temptations at every turn. Most were sanctimoniously refused, leaving just market stalls, street traders and coffee shops to benefit from our inquisitive presence, though only the latter benefited from the cash I had managed to con out of a reluctant machine with my credit card.

The railway station forecourt was packed with students, buskers, and other assorted criminals when we returned in the early evening. Large audiences encircled one or two of the most popular entertainers, causing us to walk grumpily around them, tripping over bodies and bags as we threaded our way to the main entrance. Amsterdam police could learn a lot from the heavily armed Venetian Fascist Anti-Inter-Rail Water Cannon Squads, I thought to myself, realising how much youthful idealism I had lost since my previous Inter-Rail trip.

Amsterdam meant more to me following this trip than it did the first time I offended the city with my presence. On the earlier visit, I had learned from a graffiti painting of a flasher opening his coat to an unimpressed woman that 'It ain't much if it ain't Dutch' and that the Dutch word *kunt* wasn't even remotely dirty, in any context. This time, however, Amsterdam had given more of its secrets to me. I now felt inaugurated into Dutch culture, I knew what all these well-endowed Dutchmen did on their way to work, I appreciated the finer points of Dutch cinema, and I had discovered two McDonald's that I had missed the first time. And Amsterdam had retained an important part of me, too, albeit in its fine sewer system. I left the city that night feeling that both me and it had benefited in some obscure and utterly indefensible and pointless way from my visit that day.

★

The 20:10 train to Copenhagen was Danish, so it stood out like a long, brown stool in contrast to the bright yellow Dutch trains all around it in Amsterdam Centraal. We boarded the train early enough to be able to steal a couple of signs from its interior before anyone could give us a jolly well deserved reprimanding. Paul's feet still weren't up to full strength after the unfortunate bathing incident at the weekend, but we sealed the window and door to our compartment and hung his fungal shoes close to where the head would appear of any foreign type who wanted to share with us. Our luggage was spread over the three spare seats to give the

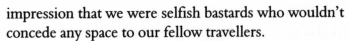

impression that we were selfish bastards who wouldn't concede any space to our fellow travellers.

Nervous minutes passed while the train began to fill with assorted scum and the odd normal person. All we could do was point our feet at the compartment door and hope for the best. Twice the door slid open, and twice the offenders wisely chose not to pursue their investigation of our unventilated sweat box. Finally, accurate to the second, the train pulled away with everyone accommodated: in the corridors, in the toilets, and bursting out of every compartment except ours.

We were, naturally, delighted with our achievement, and celebrated by removing a sticker from the window and trying to unscrew a light fitting with a penknife. The latter project was abandoned when we realised we didn't really want a light fitting, nor did we want bare live wires protruding behind our heads for the next ten hours.

The train rolled quickly and smoothly towards Holland's northern extremities, but before we could go to sleep there was an important matter to be dealt with. A large sachet of exotic herbs was still in our possession, and ought not to be by the time the border guards stormed in. Paul was studying the packet, thoughtfully.

'What are you going to do with it?' I asked. 'Put it in a condom and stick it up your arse?'

'No room,' replied Paul.

'Why don't you throw it out of the window?' suggested Alastair.

Paul ignored us both and opened the packet. He then produced a Rizla made from an entire oak tree and rolled

170

the whole stash into one bulbous joint that needed two hands to support it. I checked in the corridor to verify that there were no fascists in the immediate vicinity, and the torch was lit. Suddenly it seemed as if Eva had joined us in the compartment, so thick was the smoke. By the time the border guards joined the train, we were happily unconscious in our sleeping bags, with only a larger than average dog-end on the floor remaining as evidence.

– Sex Prefab –

STEWART

Copenhagen station has always been one of our favourite places where trains stop, where people wait and where drug addicts hassle you endlessly for money and cigarettes. Beneath all this excitement is the Inter-Rail centre, a place where five years previously (as recounted in *Don't Lean Out of the Window!*) we had boldly engraved our names in the wooden tables for the benefit of posterity. In case this wasn't enough, we had also written graffiti on all the walls and on the rest of the furniture, and helped ourselves to more than our fair share of free condoms. We were therefore extremely keen to witness our handiwork once more, to find out if anyone had responded to our stupid messages, and to see how our engravings had stood the test of time.

Things were clearly not right with the Inter-Rail centre, though. Before we had descended all of the stairs we knew things had changed. There was no bucket of free condoms welcoming you to Denmark, no grotty registration desk where you used to have to show your Inter-Rail ticket, and no bloodstains on the floor. The difference was disturbing. Our fears were confirmed upon entering the underground room: the entire place had been ruined by a complete re-fit, extending to new graffiti-proof furniture, new plastic chairs, brighter walls, better security for personal possessions and no more male access to the female washrooms. It seemed as if the Danish Inter-Rail Police had conspired to remove all traces of our visit, like a cover-up of alien landings.

172

Can't say I blame them, really.

We squeezed our three rucksacks into a locker, paid for using a coin from a little bag of useless foreign crap that we had earned on previous trips abroad. Our mission for the day was to undertake a quest for cash and burgers, rather like any other day, so we exited the station and deliberately crossed the wide, not-very-busy-at-all road where we had been fashed by a bus driver for illegal jay-walking the last time we were here. Regrettably for our stomachs, wherever we set up our guitars we managed to get fashed immediately. Shop owners, policemen and ordinary plebs all had a go at us for various reasons. I was beginning to feel that it wasn't just me who had lost all youthful idealism in recent years.

We put away our guitars and walked away from the shopping centres, out towards the touristy areas that we hadn't been to before. It was disturbingly far from any of the fast food places that we were hoping to visit later, but the long walk was the price we had to pay for our lunch (plus the Krone, of course). A quaint old bollocky cobbled street emerged beneath our feet, almost out of nowhere. We followed it round a corner to a canal with a working lock, some ice cream stalls and dozens of bored tourists. Perfect.

'This is great,' said Alastair. 'We'll make much more money here than in the town centre.'

'I'm glad we picked the lock,' I said.

The busking session was a hit, in relative terms, and we were able to head back to the civilised part of Copenhagen in time to stuff our faces and then catch the next train to Germany at 15:20. This train, however, terminated at Tåstrup as far as we were concerned. This was where the fascist threw us off for the annoyingly familiar crime of not being able to pay a supplement for standing in the corridor of a train that we had no idea required a supplement in the first place. Undeterred by this minor setback, we bodged our way out of Denmark via the 15:59 to Nykøbing, then the 17:51 from Nykøbing to Puttgarden, and finally the 19:51 train to Hamburg, arriving in good time to witness the city's widely reputed nightlife.

PAUL

It was interesting to see the site of our first experience of 'live pornography' again. It had been a few years since that eventful evening and having had to remember what it looked like for the predecessor to this book (*Don't Lean Out of the Window!*) I was curious to see how wildly swept up in hyperbole I had become when describing it. For the most part my recollection had been fairly accurate: the building looked as I had remembered it, i.e. the same size and layout and the same garish silver and blue neon sign that read 'Sex World'. On reflection, 'Sex Prefab' would probably have been more accurate.

Stewart was tempted to enter this den of depravity having been told over and over of the events which Alastair and I had experienced. I felt some sympathy for him as he had missed what had been a defining moment in our lives, and it would have been a defining moment in his life too, had he not been sat at a deserted station in Zwolle at the time being hassled by a drunk German trying to sell him drugs. Still, that's the way of things.

174

Tonight, though, we were on a pretty tight schedule if we were to catch our escape train from horrid, cold northern Europe to nice, warm central Europe and therefore we deigned that there would only be time for a four-course feast at McDonald's before we left.

We found the local outlet for two-all-beef-patties-special-sauce-lettuce-cheese-pickles-onions-in-a-sesame-seed-bun and set about ordering from the menu with typical gluttony.

'How much have we got? Enough for five each?' asked Stewart. I counted the money. We had sixty-eight marks – ample for a last feast in a country to which we would not be returning. I divided the money equally and we each ordered our own pile of balanced and nutritious food from the extensive menu. Half an hour later we were unable to move, so, incarcerated as we were in a burger restaurant, we saw fit to pass the time by eating more burgers. Time marched on, however, and after we'd each gained about 5% extra bodyweight it was time to waddle to the station.

Hamburg Hauptbahnhof is a bloody big station – I said that in the last book (it's on page 174 so if you want to know more you'd better buy that one too) and we were not disappointed by the inevitable offers of sex and requests for money: it's a shame it wasn't the other way round, really. Our train was to leave quite soon at 22:47 so we made our way briskly to the platform.

'What does that red diamond mean then?' asked Alastair. I looked up at the departures television, a triumph of German broadcasting in that it's about the only thing that isn't dubbed from American.

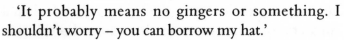

'It probably means no gingers or something. I shouldn't worry – you can borrow my hat.'

'Wanker!'

The train arrived from a nearby siding and was immediately invaded by swarms of Inter-Railers and other pond life. We roamed up and down the corridors for a quarter of an hour looking for some space to dump ourselves and our considerable amount of crap. We could see a fascist coming down the compartment checking tickets but thought nothing of it.

'Fahrkarten!'

I produced the Inter-Rail tickets on behalf of the others while the fascist examined them with a look of disdain. *'Vier und zwanzig mark!'* he added, proffering his hand in an upside-down Nazi salute. We'd been caught again: on a Hun-train that needed a supplement. We rummaged around our collective pockets, wallets and rucksack compartments but could only muster twenty-two marks. We couldn't believe it – sunk by one cheeseburger's worth of Teutonic currency. The fascist was typically unrelenting in his approach. He was determined to throw us off at the earliest opportunity despite our offers of Visa, MasterCard or the chance to scrounge the two mark shortfall from our fellow passengers. Thus we were unceremoniously ejected at Hamburg-Harburg – a nowhere station on the southern outskirts of the city.

'Fucking wanker!' shouted Alastair at the fascist as the train accelerated out of the station.

A quick examination of the timetable revealed that if we were going to go to München as we had intended then a six hour wait on the platform would be involved.

While that is just tolerable in France and Italy there was no way we were hanging about in the freezing night in northern Germany. A couple of minutes later we were on another train headed for Stuttgart.

'That's where Mercedes come from,' Stewart pointlessly informed us.

– MUSICAL NAZI FANTASYLAND –

STEWART

Despite the thrill of being in a city that manufactures cars whose owners refuse to think of them ever being 'second hand', regardless of the number of changes of ownership, in much the same way that a rusty Picasso painting with dodgy wheel bearings and a leaking oil sump would never be called second hand, we decided to leave Stuttgart after a full minute at the station. A nearby platform offered us a passage to Salzburg, departing at 09:17, so we hopped on and sat in its stuffy corridor all morning, jealously moaning about the wankers who had planned their journey to Salzburg more than a minute in advance and hence had arrived early enough to get seats.

We spent an hour wandering the streets of Salzburg, looking in shop windows at miniature Mozart figurines, boxes of souvenir Mozart chocolates, and bottles of synthesized Mozart piss, before it clicked that this city probably had some kind of connection with the decomposing composer. We had no Austrian currency and needed to busk to pay for our late breakfast of croissants shaped like Mozart's crack, but the piano insignia, the endless Mozart souvenirs, indeed the very fabric of the city seemed to be against us, denying the existence of popular music, and defying anyone to suggest that music other than by Mozzy was still music. The local people would appreciate our busking about as much as we would enjoy sitting on a spike and listening to Mozart's complete works played on the jam jars.

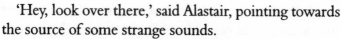

'Hey, look over there,' said Alastair, pointing towards the source of some strange sounds.

We had just left a narrow medieval shopping street and were now in a wide, open square, probably called Mozart Square, along one side of which was the front wall to a large palace, probably called Mozart's Privy. In the centre of this square was a small crowd gathered around the busker who was causing the weird noises. He had about a hundred water-filled jam jars in a semi-circle around him, and was hitting them with a pair of drumsticks.

'It's one of Mozart's sonatas,' said Alastair, having decoded the seemingly random chink-chinks and pop-pops. 'Let's sit over here and watch.'

We walked closer to the busker and sat on concrete bollards that were so thin they seemed eager to work their way into our underwear. The music droned on, and so did Alastair.

'It's one of his later pieces. The trills in the first coda then give way to a run of upper and lower mordents that build to a slow crescendo in the final movement ending with a chink of the half-pint jam jar.'

In far corners of the square, other buskers were playing Mozart on more conventional instruments like washboards and buckets. With our refreshing brand of guitar-based pop we stood to make a fortune.

'Let's go and busk back in one of those shopping streets,' I said.

'Would that be Mozart Street, perchance?' asked Paul.

'That's the chap.'

There was a shallow alcove in the street, between a piano shop and a Mozart café. We set up in this miniature

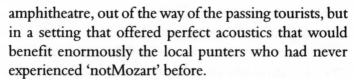
amphitheatre, out of the way of the passing tourists, but in a setting that offered perfect acoustics that would benefit enormously the local punters who had never experienced 'notMozart' before.

'I'm going to tell aunt Mary about uncle John, he said he had the bizzy but he got a lot of fun, oh baby!' we yelled, thrashing out our best twelve bar rock 'n' roll number, inventing gibberish where we didn't know the words, and filling the street to the rafters with our joyous cacophony. A man in a shop opposite quickly looked in his Encyclopaedia of Mozart to see where this unusually noisy ditty had come from. He looked puzzled, and then confused, and then angry as he realised that this was the fabled 'notMozart' of which he had lived in ignorant fear all of his life.

Whether he called the police at this point, I'll never know, but very quickly a couple of fascists arrived and told us to stop our heretical music.

'That is not Mozart you have been playing, is it?' asked the taller fascist with a long, thin moustache that mirrored his shape. He looked down at us in a patronising manner.

'Er, no,' I replied. 'That was Little Richard.'

'We only allow musicians to play Mozart in Salzburg,' explained the other fascist.

'We could try *Roll Over Beethoven*,' said Alastair.

'You are not classical musicians,' said the first fascist.

'I'm not a musician at all,' protested Paul.

'We cannot allow you to play here. The tourists expect Mozart. You are bad for the economy.'

Not half as bad as the fascists were to our own little economy. We packed up and searched for somewhere to change our foreign coins so that we could eat. This exchange generated enough Schillings for a late breakfast/ early lunch of Mozart flavour crisps and bread, following by indigestion.

'What's your opinion of Mozart?' Alastair asked Paul as we headed back to the station.

'I think most art is crap. Most of it was only painted because they didn't have cameras, so there's no excuse for art at all these days now we've all got photographic equipment coming out of our arses.'

'I meant *Mozart*, the composer.'

'Oh, you meant Mozart with italicised emphasis? What do I think of him?'

'Yes.'

'I think he's dead.'

'Oh.'

'And crap.'

PAUL

Though the landscape through which we passed en route to Kitzbühel during the late afternoon was undoubtedly scenic, we were sick of it. We'd become spoilt by a surfeit of beautiful scenery and diverse culture so our collective thoughts converged on the one unifying entity: McDonald's. The others had been to Kitzbühel before and they assured themselves and me that we could look forward to the indubitable culinary excellence of this establishment on our arrival.

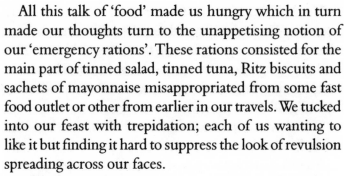

All this talk of 'food' made us hungry which in turn made our thoughts turn to the unappetising notion of our 'emergency rations'. These rations consisted for the main part of tinned salad, tinned tuna, Ritz biscuits and sachets of mayonnaise misappropriated from some fast food outlet or other from earlier in our travels. We tucked into our feast with trepidation; each of us wanting to like it but finding it hard to suppress the look of revulsion spreading across our faces.

After the rations we became bored again. I leaned out of the window and smoked a cigarette as Alastair gave us a convincing impersonation of a French teenager by performing feats of gymnastic mastery while suspending himself ape-like from grab rails that hung down from the ceiling.

I must have been dozing as we arrived at Kitzbühel because the memory of our approach is non-existent. I remember being shaken roughly and shouted at by the others and the next thing I can remember was that the train was gone and we were alone at a station whose sign did not read 'Kitzbühel'. Still, I was assured by the others that this was indeed the correct station to alight at because they had been to Kitzbühel before, though how they knew the station when last time they arrived by car is beyond me. We left the station and joined a 'main' road. Stewart pointed to a distant settlement halfway up the alpine slopes.

'That might be Kitzbühel,' he proclaimed, without conviction.

★

The heat was still uncomfortable even though it was late afternoon and I was trying to reconcile to myself the fact that the Austrian railway planners of yesteryear had built a station so far from the town it was supposed to serve. The houses were brightly painted and built in typical alpine style. My mind filled with hideous spectres of the von Trapp family singing in their sickly saccharine sweet voices. 'Ooooh, laaa, laaa. We're living in Nazi occupied Europe and everything is just dandy,' they sang. 'Let's pick some flowers. Mind the barbed wire there!'

I resurfaced from musical Nazi fantasyland as we rounded a corner on one of the main streets into town. In front of us, the fire brigade was busy putting out a building. That's right: not a fire, but a building. Admittedly, the building was not as well maintained as all the others but I didn't really think it warranted the firemen kicking the doors in, breaking the windows and emptying gallons of water into it. We observed this drill for a few minutes and must have looked as bemused as we were because a man came up to us and informed us that the brigade was practising for a real fire. After a few minutes, the firemen had had enough and the fire hoses went limp as the engine master turned off the pumps. This didn't seem to bother Alastair however as he had by this point stripped to the waist and was signalling to the firemen that he needed a shower. We all did in fact.

Obligingly, one of them re-opened a valve and a torrent of water sprang forth. Alastair caught the full force of the jet in the chest and stumbled backwards a couple of steps. Regaining his balance he went through his high

pressure ablutions in front of an audience of over one hundred.

With the fire brigade's odd practice over with and the crowd dispersed, it occurred to us that we should decide on busking tactics for the rest of the day. Personally I wasn't interested in busking: I just wanted a beer, a snack and somewhere to doss down for the night.

'We should busk down there,' dictated Alastair, pointing towards the town centre. Not that it was much of a town centre you understand – more a pedestrianised road with a couple of bars, a shop and a bank on it. Stewart looked at me despairingly.

'Can't we just get an advance on your Visa card?' asked Stewart with more optimism than was appropriate.

'No way,' said Alastair as he pulled on a 'fresh' shirt from his rucksack. 'We can't afford it.'

Stewart and I volunteered to go and scope out the town for the best pitch while Alastair finished tarting himself up. Round the corner and out of sight of miser-boy we conspired to withdraw some money from a nearby cashpoint that was calling to us. We only withdrew 100 Schillings which was about five quid but Alastair was right: we couldn't afford it, really. But at least we had some back-up funds now.

We set up a pitch in the main street next to a wooden news-stand that was shut and boarded up for the night. Some of the clientele from the nearby bars eyed us quizzically. We reassured ourselves that they had not seen buskers before, such was Kitzbühel's status as a town full of toffee-nosed, rich, Tory-voting skiers and bon viveurs. Having lined ourselves up in the correct order, i.e. Stewart and his enormous smile in the middle and the more dour Alastair and myself on either side for symmetry, we started banging out a few chords. Or notes in my case. Alright, note. Almost immediately people started coming forward and dropping coins into the hat. Our morale boosted, we stepped up the pace of the songs and soon money was raining down from all directions. Much of it was going nowhere near the hat at all as many members of the audience remained seated at their outside bar tables and were simply tossing what spare change they had at us.

'Fuck!' exclaimed Stewart at a point in the song where I normally expected him to be singing 'Oooooh'. 'That coin just hit my strumming hand,' he explained while Alastair and I attempted to keep in time with one another. It was obvious we would have to be more vigilant from now on, and the rest of the set was spent half smiling inanely and singing, and half scanning the bar terraces for high velocity coinage heading in our direction.

A barmaid with enormous cleavage marched over to us with three glasses of beer. She set them down on a window ledge behind us and gestured that they were for us and then pointed to a gentleman with an odd Australian-style bush hat and a suspiciously large moustache. As we looked at him he raised his glass as if to say 'Cheers!'. We nervously acknowledged him by raising our glasses in reply.

'He better not be after a shag,' Alastair threatened under his breath.

After forty minutes and three encores we were allowed to stop playing. We were not used to being this popular

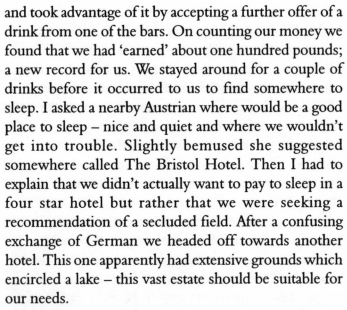

and took advantage of it by accepting a further offer of a drink from one of the bars. On counting our money we found that we had 'earned' about one hundred pounds; a new record for us. We stayed around for a couple of drinks before it occurred to us to find somewhere to sleep. I asked a nearby Austrian where would be a good place to sleep – nice and quiet and where we wouldn't get into trouble. Slightly bemused she suggested somewhere called The Bristol Hotel. Then I had to explain that we didn't actually want to pay to sleep in a four star hotel but rather that we were seeking a recommendation of a secluded field. After a confusing exchange of German we headed off towards another hotel. This one apparently had extensive grounds which encircled a lake – this vast estate should be suitable for our needs.

The walk to the lake was not by any stretch the two kilometres I had been assured it was. We were all becoming more sweaty and irritable than usual, shuffling our rucksacks around trying to make them sit more comfortably. About forty minutes after we had set off on our two kilometre hike we came upon the perimeter fence of the hotel. Making our way along it until we found a gate we were greeted by a message which I almost understood. The salient points were: private, strictly for guests, no access to anywhere other than the hotel and that trespassers would be shot in the throat using a high velocity rifle. Or something. Undeterred we let ourselves in and skirted the perimeter of the lake looking for somewhere out of rifle range of the hotel.

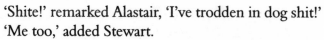

'Shite!' remarked Alastair, 'I've trodden in dog shit!'

'Me too,' added Stewart.

I thought I may had done too, but kept quiet.

Stewart rummaged around one of his many storage areas and produced a Maglite. Closer examination revealed that rather than all three of us simultaneously stepping in excrement, we had in fact all walked into the outskirts of a swamp.

'Shite!' Alastair exclaimed again. 'I've been bitten now.' Stewart directed the beam of his torch upwards to reveal an airborne soup of mosquitoes. We all decided that sleeping in a swamp being bitten by insects with the added risk of sniper attack was not an attractive proposition. We hurriedly left by the gate we had entered and set off down the road. By this point we had endured enough and would sleep anywhere. Breaking through some undergrowth we emerged in a dell at the end of a field. Silently and despondently we dragged our sleeping bags out of our rucksacks and laid them out on the grass under some trees. A few minutes later I broke the silence to remind the others that my sleeping bag had a waterproof base to it and theirs didn't. There was no reply.

'Wanker!' volunteered Alastair a few minutes later.

– Bruce Forsyth –

Stewart

I've slept rough in many parts of Europe. My natural instinct is always to find a site that's well secluded, affording a safe, peaceful night's sleep without the embarrassment of public scrutiny upon waking up, desperate for a pee, with a morning salute trying to burst out of the sleeping bag. Last night's decision to sleep in the middle of a remote field seemed to fulfil all the necessary criteria for an undisturbed morning. Predictably, therefore, we found ourselves woken up at six by the sound of heavy machinery and sprightly workmen intent upon laying a road through us.

They showed no emotion as we hopped out of the way in our sleeping bags in order to let their destructive convoy through. Indeed, they appeared fully accustomed to this type of obstruction. At the bottom of the field was gathered a collection of lorries, vans and cement mixers, one of which was fitted with a kind of scraping device for removing sleeping Inter-Railers from the route of the new road.

We packed up quickly, avoiding the sleeping-Inter-Railer-removing-machine, and lolloped half-asleep into the centre of Kitzbühel. At breakfast, we were delighted by servings of orange juice that were big enough to go scuba diving in. McDonald's was empty apart from ourselves and a group of Austrian girls, next to whom we sat in a typically unsubtle manner.

'Excuse me,' said one of them, leaning over towards our table, 'do you have a fire?' She pointed at her unlit cigarette.

Alastair responded on our behalves, despite not yet having woken up.

'Only in my pants for you, darling,' he offered.

If it had been possible to tap the chill that instantly filled her eyes, we could have delayed global warming by a few decades. Fridge manufacturers would have been bankrupted by her icy glare, her supercooled disdain for us, and her handy freezer compartment. We were struck down by her frosty look, frozen solid by her hatred of our cheap, schoolboyish and sexist ways.

'I think you're in there, mate!' Paul told Alastair.

'Yeah, go for it,' I said, from beneath the table.

★

Yesterday's busking cash was still plentiful after a night of budget accommodation, but there were many days' travel ahead of us, and it was always prudent to milk a lucrative site dry before moving on. We set up in the same place as the previous evening, but had earned little more than a bag of assorted groceries kindly selected for us by a local woman when we were fashed.

'You boys,' said the fascist, 'you boys must have a licence to play.'

For some reason, he reminded me of a Teutonic Roger.

'I cannot let you boys play until you get a licence from the Mayor. That is his office across the street.'

Licensed busking somehow seemed to go against the whole point of it. What we did was meant to be illegal, uncontrolled by the local breadheads. We preferred to get in and out of a town with all their cash before anyone noticed that we had no musical skills. Getting the approval of a fat, tone-deaf Nazi for our busking enterprise was anathema to us. We were part of the underworld, we were a sub-culture, we were black marketeers. We lived at the edge of society, unwashed, unregulated, and untalented. That was busking in its purest form.

Paul spoke the best German (compared to us, not to Germans), so he was volunteered to ask the Mayor for a licence.

Some minutes later, he returned; his expression giving no clues as to the outcome of his negotiations.

'Yes, we can have a licence,' he told us.

'That's great!' I said.

'Yeah – we can make a fortune,' said Alastair.

'Yes, we can have a licence,' repeated Paul, 'but it will take three days to process.'

'Arse,' I said.

That was the end of our busking in Kitzbühel. I looked in the brown paper bag of food that had been donated to us, and identified some bananas, a loaf of bread, and some chocolate. I pocketed the chocolate.

★

One of the problems of international travel is the sheer diversity of the laws that apply from place to place. It's impossible to be aware of every local law, and yet ignorance is never a defence, even when ignorance of most things so obviously applies to Inter-Railers. We had been in Austria for two entire days before we discovered that we could very easily have committed a particularly despicable offence, the existence of which no one had warned us about.

We learnt of this statutory crime upon arrival at Kitzbühel's park. A sign graphically depicted a number of examples of antisocial behaviour that had been outlawed, and most of these crimes were familiar to us: running, being a dog, and making love. But one of the activities prohibited suggested this was a land living under a stricter moral code than any self-disrespecting Inter-Railer could cope with. The sign depicted Bruce Forsyth in sideways silhouette, one leg cocked behind him and one hand curled towards his forehead in 'thoughtful' pose, just as he had stood for some moments every week in the seventies before his forty minute tirade of catchphrases, loosely disguised as a game show. The sign didn't make clear whether phrases such as 'Give us a twirl, Anthea' or 'Didn't she do well?' were prosecutable, or whether it was only a crime to assume the banned one's pose. Or to possess an infeasibly large chin.

After a bout of illegal Bruce Forsyth impersonations beneath the sign, for the benefit of our photo albums, we were feeling thoroughly reckless and irresponsible. But we had to calm down a little. It was time to show some sensitivity towards these poor Austrians. They had been through a lot, what with losing the war and subsequently being force-fed dubbed editions of *The Generation Game* as part of the punishment. It was all very well reminding them, at every available opportunity, that they lost the war, but acting out Bruce Forsyth

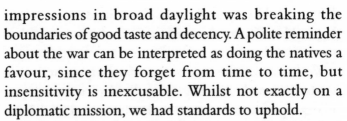

impressions in broad daylight was breaking the boundaries of good taste and decency. A polite reminder about the war can be interpreted as doing the natives a favour, since they forget from time to time, but insensitivity is inexcusable. Whilst not exactly on a diplomatic mission, we had standards to uphold.

'Are my nads showing through my trousers?' asked Alastair, pointing to the rip in his Indian hippie trousers through which one of his testicles was trying to see something of the world.

'Nah. Barely,' I said, sitting down on a bench adjacent to a decorative fountain, the centre piece of the little park. 'It's the trousers that cause the most offence, anyway. Have you got anything else clean?'

'I'm going to sort my shit out,' interrupted Paul.

'Me too. See if I can throw some stuff away,' I said.

We all began to delve into the dustbins we had been carrying on our backs for the last couple of weeks, pulling out unidentifiable objects and attempting to give them names. With many days of travel ahead of us, I was determined to reduce the weight on my back. The electric shaver I carried contained enough charge for the remainder of the trip, and yet I was carrying two power cords for it. Neither of which worked very well. The longest of the two was the first thing to be thrown away. It was closely followed by empty plastic bags, an assortment of dirty socks and an embarrassing long-out-of-fashion T-shirt. We weren't planning on camping anymore, so out went the plastic airbed that gave me backache and a rusty little gas stove.

With a reasonably large pile of stuff thrown away, my rucksack was noticeably lighter. I felt like performing a brief Rodney Dangerfield impression by way of celebration, but although such acts were not specifically outlawed, I thought it best to err on the cautious side.

'Gee,' I said, neglecting to complete the catchphrase, thereby rendering it unprosecutable.

The others hadn't thrown much away, but they had each assembled a considerably unpleasant quantity of dirty washing, and had resolved to walk to the river to get it cleaned. We had no chance of getting away with polluting the pure water cascading over the rockpool in this park, so we hiked to the edge of town where the river was accessible via a slippery, muddy slope bordering a car park.

Like washerwomen on the banks of the Ganges we stripped off our tops and scrubbed away at our clothes on the smooth rocks. Except Indian washerwomen probably didn't strip off. And we weren't on the banks of the Ganges. After a brief interval, during which we evacuated the water in order to let Paul's excrescence float safely downstream, we finished off washing everything apart from the boxer shorts in which we stood, and rigged up a washing line in the adjacent trees.

It was a hot day, but clouds were brewing on the horizon. If the clothes didn't dry before nightfall, they would fester and mould in our bags until we remembered to hang them out again in another country, by which time they would be in exactly the same condition as before we washed them. Besides which, we would have to wear wet clothes tonight, and that wouldn't do: tonight we were going to the pub.

Alastair was across the street at the telephone box when the first shower fell. Paul and I grabbed the clothes from off the line and bundled them into the appropriate rucksacks, then went to sit under the porch of the car park's public toilet wearing only moist shorts and wet, clinging shirts. I considered holding all my clothes out one by one under the hot air hand dryer in the toilet, but that would be a last resort. If any were dropped into the piss they would have to be washed again. Eventually. Electric drying was a last resort, just to be used for the essential clothes required for when we went to the pub tonight. The rain fell more heavily now, splashing warm droplets from a large puddle onto our bare legs.

There was no way our stuff was going to get dry today. I imagined us dangling our damp boxer shorts and socks on the luggage racks on our next train, dripping river water onto the heads of angry fellow passengers. It served us right, I supposed, for deviating from the true traditions of Inter-Rail, which were not to wash at all for a month. Still, the holiday couldn't get much worse.

'I got some bad news, guys,' said Alastair, splashing us again, unaware of the rain. 'My results arrived today. Apparently I didn't pass one of the papers.'

'Which one?' asked Paul.

'Subcutaneous and Soft Tissue Medicine.'

'That's lard, isn't it?' translated Paul.

'Yeah, lard. I was bloody close, too.'

'That's put a bit of a Belgium on the European map of your academic record,' said Paul. 'That was a sort of

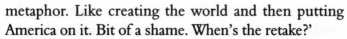

metaphor. Like creating the world and then putting America on it. Bit of a shame. When's the retake?'

'Three weeks from now.'

'So you'll have a whole week to revise after we get back,' I suggested.

'Yes, but that won't be long enough. There's a lot to know about lard, and if I don't pass this paper I can't finish the degree.'

'Think what a blow that would be to the world of medicine,' warned Paul.

'I can't afford to take any chances with this. I'll have to go home tomorrow. I'm sorry.'

'But what about the rest of Europe? We've got so many more countries to criticise, cities to pollute and people to annoy. Paul and I can't busk without you: you're the musical one. We'll starve on our own.'

'I suppose that's our fault for not inheriting any musical genes. Or maybe it's Alastair's fault for not inheriting the specific genes for lard revision,' said Paul.

We tried persuading him, we tried arguing with him, we tried to bribe him; but all was to no avail. No matter what reasons we put forward, there was no way we could persuade him to leave any sooner than the next morning. Only joshing. Unforeseen circumstances had therefore forced this to be our last night together, and we were determined to make the most of it with a night of decadence in the town's English pub, followed by another shivery night of homelessness.

The landlord of the pub was a chirpy British type, unimpressed by our presence even though we were amazed to meet another person who was familiar with

195

the Queen's tongue. The peak time of year for this establishment was the winter season, when the pub would be filled with drunken hoity-toity skiers, irritating photos of whom – shouting 'rah-rah' and waving huge wads of cash – were stuck to the walls.

We piled our crap into a corner of the bar, ordered a round of minuscule, cheap beers, and wondered how Paul and myself could fund two more weeks of travelling when we would have to busk with only two guitars, one shaky voice and a large dose of self-consciousness. There was no way. The only option was to mug Alastair for all he was worth before he left, and to extract every last drip of fluidity from my credit card.

'If only you hadn't been blacklisted from getting any credit at all, anywhere in the world, ever,' I said to Paul.

'Lend us some Schillings,' he answered.

When the beers were gone in the first mouthfuls, we had a meeting to discuss whether we could afford a second round, or whether we should go outside to the nearest drinking fountain, fill up our water bottles, and bemoan our poverty.

'Sod it,' I said. 'Me and Paul are going to Eastern Europe next. They only earn a potato a day, unless they're doctors or pilots or something. Then they get broccoli too.'

'The Prime Minister gets Spam,' added Paul.

'So we won't need much money. So let's drink.'

Three more quarter litres of lager arrived, courtesy of *Alastair's Last Night Before Revision Drinking Fund*, which he had just set up, and which was now empty. As he sat down, I noticed a gorgeous Dutch girl enter the pub, with what looked like her boyfriend and her parents.

She wore a short red dress, which matched her long hair, and which clung tightly to her seventeen year old Dutch body. What the hell, I thought, risking a cheeky smile at her.

Nothing happened. I tried to hide my embarrassed face behind the tiny beer glass. The four of them sat at the opposite corner of the pub, all in a line on a padded pew. Still no response from her. Then her boyfriend stood up to get the first round in. As soon as he was facing away from her, she shot a huge smile across the room to me. I nudged the others to gain verification for my score, but Paul pleaded ignorance and Alastair said she was probably smiling at him.

To prove that her smile had not been accidental, coincidental, or merely the result of a nervous disorder, I caught her eye again and winked exaggeratedly. This caused her to raise her eyebrows as if she were auditioning to be Roger Moore's understudy.

'Did you see that?' I checked with the sceptical duo.

'See what?' asked Alastair.

As the evening progressed I couldn't help looking through the ever-thickening crowd in the room across to this Dutch girl. It was obvious from her demeanour that her relationship with her boyfriend had problems (aside from me). He spoke frequently to her, but received only the kind of monosyllabic replies you'd get from questioning a footballer. I deduced that this was a holiday romance that had already soured. It was not an opportunity to be missed.

After some moments of mental agony, I came to a decision.

'I'm just going outside,' I said to the chaps. 'I may be some time.'

The Dutch girl smiled at me again as I approached her en route to the door. I flicked my head towards the door, subtly inviting her to join me outside. I didn't think she would have the audacity to follow me, but I had forgotten that Dutch girls study How To Cheat On Your Boyfriend Under His Nose from the age of 12 at school, so she would have had about five years' experience in this field.

Outside it was drizzling again. I stretched my arms and enjoyed the refreshing coolness of the water on my face. I strolled across the empty street and back, then sat on a low brick wall.

And waited.

How long should I give it before I admit defeat and return to the pub, I wondered? Long enough to work out a convincing explanation as to why I chose to stand outside in the rain on my own instead of sitting in a nice, warm pub. But before I could formulate anything remotely palatable the Dutch beauty stepped outside and joined me in all her full-bodied splendour.

'Hello,' she said, somehow having managed to identify me as English.

'*Hoi*,' I said, just to throw her.

She then spoke gibberish quickly and excitedly until I told her that, unfortunately, her first impressions of me had been correct.

'This is very strange, isn't it?'

'Maybe,' she said.

'Is that your boyfriend inside?'

'Oh, him. Yes. He is going back to Holland tomorrow. I don't like him, but my parents think he's cute.'

'Oh.'

'I'm Angelique.'

'You took the words right out of my mouth,' I said, Sid James style.

'I live in Hoogeveen. In Holland.'

'I'm Poo. Shall we kiss, then?'

'OK.'

It was a brief snog, but laced with passion and a thrilling sense of danger. We agreed to meet again later that night, once her boyfriend had gone to his hotel.

Back in the pub, I walked awkwardly past the cuck-olded youngster and across to the incredulous faces of Paul and Alastair. They were attempting to lick the last residues of beer from the insides of their glasses before giving up.

'Have you just done what I think you've just done?' asked Paul.

'Farted?'

'I mean with that bird over there. You've both been out in the rain together. Tell me you didn't score . . .'

I milked the situation for all it was worth (about three Schillings in local currency), trying to avoid the subject of when we should leave the bar. I wanted to stick around until closing time, whenever that was.

'You're such a bastard,' observed Alastair, with a hint of admiration.

'True,' I admitted, 'but it takes two to tango.'

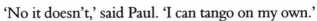

'No it doesn't,' said Paul. 'I can tango on my own.'

In order to be able to remain in the bar a little longer I bought another round, and dished it out with strict instructions to drink slowly. Paul consumed it in one quick gulp, and Alastair wasn't far behind. They had decided to go back to a bridge near the park under which we could sleep, adjacent to a bubbling stream. They took my guitar for me in addition to their own crap, in order to free an extra arm for sundry groping purposes.

I sat alone for a few minutes, catching Angelique's eye at every opportunity, patiently waiting for her ex-boyfriend to go to bed. I could tell she was dropping subtle hints to him like *'why don't you just fuck off, Dutch boy, I want to get frisky with that scummy Inter-Railer in the corner'*. Whatever it was she said, he soon left.

'Where are you staying, Poo?' she asked me, outside once more.

'We've got a place over by the park. Next to a river.'

'Are you all sharing together?'

'You could say that, yes.'

'I share a room with my parents in a hotel. I'm sorry I can't invite you back.'

'Not as sorry as I am.'

We walked towards the park together, hand-in-hand, as if we actually knew each other. I would have preferred to have been arm-in-arm with her given the damp chill in the air, but my rucksack would only have made that possible with a chimpanzee, an experience that would have to wait.

Outside the park we stopped under a bus shelter. Angelique's face was lit by a weak street lamp that accentuated her beauty and turned her freckles into a homogenous dark tan. Rain battered the tin roof above us, muffling our speech. I put down the rucksack and pulled her towards me. Our hands found their ways into each other's clothing, seeking erogenous warmth.

'We must meet tomorrow evening,' she said. 'I will be free then.'

'Oh, you mean I'm paying for tonight?'

'My boyfriend will be gone. It would be nice to get together for a few days.'

It certainly would. But our plans for the conquest of Europe required us to leave Kitzbühel the next day, soon after Alastair was due to leave for home and his clever books about lard. Austria wasn't a cheap place to live, even when you're living illegally, and we needed to get to a less prosperous part of the world before our dubiously-earned cash ran out. Besides, it wasn't fair to leave Paul on his own while I frolicked with this young lady. He would be forced to try earning a living from only his bass guitar, the prospect of which was too horrible to contemplate. To be fair, he could keep a bass solo going for an hour at a push – two hours if he learned a second note – but I couldn't see it going down too well with the locals.

Our affair was destined from the start to be a brief one. We didn't even bother to swap addresses. We were just like two ships that passed in the night. Or rather, ships that stopped to board each other for a snog, then continued on their way.

I gave her a long kiss goodnight, then hauled on my rucksack and went to look for the bridge. It was a flat concrete bridge bearing a raised single lane road over the stream. Underneath it was a gravel footpath adjacent to the stream. The gravel was dry, and at least we were out of the rain. There were two long, dark shapes on the ground.

'Did you get them in, Poo?' asked one of them.

'Get what in?'

'Them. All of them. Any of them. I don't know,' elaborated Alastair's voice.

I put on some more damp clothes and unrolled my sleeping bag, laying it up against the padded case that contained my guitar and which was to become my pillow. Then I climbed inside, warming the interior with my breath, and fell sound asleep until the violent thunderstorm some hours later woke us all up and threatened to wash us away.

– WHO DO YOU THINK YOU ARE KIDDING MR HITLER? –

PAUL

We awoke to find ourselves not only unmolested but completely dry. The torrent of water that was still sweeping down the alpine park on its exciting and eventful journey to somewhere else had risen to within an inch of the river bank, then stabilised. I had no idea what time it was but the air had a delicious fresh smell about it and the birds were chirping in the trees overhead. Half in a daze I became aware of someone's approach. Cranking my neck around as far as it would go I caught sight of a tall, slim man striding down the hill towards us. I eyed him fearfully, fully expecting to receive a bollocking. To my relief and perplexity he continued his striding gait down the hill past us. I had made eye contact with the man but he didn't seem in the least bit bothered. The others weren't awake at this point so I stopped craning my neck to see what the man was doing and lay back down.

A few minutes had passed when I heard the same footsteps coming back. I immediately feared that the man had merely ignored us until he had mustered some reinforcements from town. I needn't have worried though – he had simply been into town to fetch his newspaper. Actually, as the man grew nearer I could make out the paper's masthead. It was *The Telegraph*. The others were awake by now and glanced around at me as if to say 'You speak German. You can receive this impending bollocking on our behalves'. No bollocking was

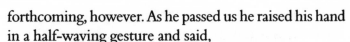

forthcoming, however. As he passed us he raised his hand in a half-waving gesture and said,

'Morning, gentlemen.'

What a civilised place this was, I decided.

★

Having got up, packed away and dispensed with the traditional, early morning insults, we resolved to make one last busking sortie in the town before Alastair fucked off back to Blighty. That way, he would have enough money for food and pornography on his solo homeward journey while Stewart and I would have enough to buy a small castle in Hungary. Probably.

We made our way down the slopes of the park full of bonhomie and into the main pedestrian precinct where we hoped to make another fortune. Alastair stopped in his tracks.

'Listen. I don't believe it!'

'Shit!' added Stewart helpfully.

'What?' I enquired. The others ignored me and made their way up the street towards the sound they were both so upset about but that I could not even hear. 'What?' I demanded. 'What is the problem?'

'Fucking pygmy bastards!' was Alastair's reply.

'Yeah! Bastard pygmies,' added Stewart, helpful as ever. There must have been a lull in the crowd noise at this point, as the sound they were mentioning became perfectly and horrifically obvious. Through the throng of tourists drifted what someone from the Ron-Tel record company might describe as: 'The haunting sound of the Andes'. What we would describe it as would be something more akin to 'Fucking samey old bollocks from dagos with pan-pipes and oversized guitars'. Our position as 'Busker Kings of the Tyrol' had been usurped by the 'Stunted, Long-Haired Bastards of South America'. We were completely unprepared for this eventuality, and stood staring at them in dismay and disbelief. One of them saw us and, recognising us also as buskers, beamed broadly and tipped us a friendly nod. This was a red rag to a bull as far as Alastair was concerned, so Stewart and I gently coaxed Alastair in the opposite direction in order that we may defuse him safely.

Alastair was not easy to console. In the end we had to concede that he was indeed correct in his theory that Dr Mengele had escaped the advancing allied troops at the end of the war and fled to Peru where he was afforded the protection of a neutral country while he continued his gruesome human cloning experiments, the results of which were now plain to see. Nutter.

Accepting that there was no more money to be made that day we walked down to the station. Alastair's train was due first. He was going to Zurich and then Frankfurt so we waited at the station with him until he left.

STEWART

It was odd seeing Alastair disappear towards home, leaving us alone on a strange and slightly smelly platform. He was pissed off at having to go back, and we were pissed off at losing him from our invasion plans. We parted in a stilted, sombre mood, cursing the pointlessness of exams that get in the way of having a

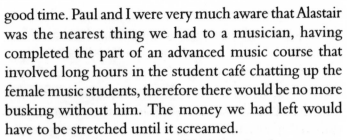

good time. Paul and I were very much aware that Alastair was the nearest thing we had to a musician, having completed the part of an advanced music course that involved long hours in the student café chatting up the female music students, therefore there would be no more busking without him. The money we had left would have to be stretched until it screamed.

With Alastair gone, we decided that for the next part of our exploration it would be cool to visit a war zone, armed only with guitars and factor five sun cream. Prices were bound to be cheap in Yugoslavia because generally wars attract zero holidaymakers. Strangely, despite the depletion of our forces by one third, this plan did not seem to us as stupid as it actually was. It was almost like a game of Russian roulette: we were going to choose a random destination somewhere in Yugoslavia without any knowledge of where the dangerous parts were. The first stage of this foolhardy excursion involved travelling on the 12:27 train to Graz, from where we would be able to pick up a supply train heading for the front line, or something.

PAUL

We surmised from the view from the train windows as we trundled through Graz's suburbs that this was a town we would not be making the effort of leaving the station to visit. The late afternoon sun was still quite high in the sky. We tried to find the cleanest part of the platform, slipped our rucksacks off our sweat-soaked backs and then dumped ourselves down on a nearby bench.

Neither of us spoke for a few minutes. I was secretly having reservations about going to Yugoslavia – yes, it was only to Zagreb, which wasn't exactly the front line, but there was definitely a risk involved and I was attempting to make a case in my own mind for taking that risk. I don't know what Stewart was thinking. I'd like to think that he was also worried though he wasn't letting it show. I was supposed to be the irresponsible one (not to mention the talentless one). It was I that was supposed to incite the others to do things that we would probably live to regret yet I somehow felt that Stewart had stolen my thunder a little and this excursion was to be his little project. A bead of sweat ran down my forehead and started to weave its way through my eyebrow. This broke me out of my period of silent contemplation and I looked around for something else to occupy my overheated mind.

A long way down the platform to our left I could make out a stainless steel trolley on castors which was attended by a man in some kind of uniform. I could also make out a Coke logo on the side of the trolley. I pointed this out to Stewart and we agreed that two cold cans would help our sweaty predicament though they were unlikely to help the odour situation. We found some Schillings and Stewart sauntered off up the platform to make his purchase. My mind wandered off on an engineering tangent connected with the question of whether I would ever be able to understand polar second moment of area when Stewart arrived back in front of me looking distinctly worried.

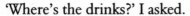

'Where's the drinks?' I asked.

'I couldn't do it. I'm frightened.'

I was bemused by this comment and my mind started rattling through possible causes for Stewart's fear.

'The bloke at the trolley is frightening. He's . . . he's Adolf Hitler!'

I considered this to be highly unlikely as it would have made the drinks seller about 103 years old, plus somebody would probably have recognised him by now. Stewart persuaded me to accompany him down the platform for a second look at this apparition.

As we approached the man I noticed that he was slightly portly and about 45 years old. I started silently slagging Stewart off for being such a ponce until we wheeled round to face the drinks seller to make a purchase. There, in front of us, was none other than Adolf Schickelgruber. I assumed that Hitler must have reverted to his original name for tax purposes but there he was – as sure as I'm writing this. Dozens of fleeting thoughts dashed through my mind in a matter of seconds. 'Surely this man must know he looks like Hitler?' my mind hypothesised. 'He must do: it's not just the hair and the psycho eyes but he must meticulously trim that moustache every morning. It can't be an accident.'

Hitler let his head fall to one side and he viewed us quizzically through narrowed eyes as if to ask if we were actually interested in buying something. I imagined all the cans to be full of Zyklon B poison gas.

'Zwei bosen Coca-cola bitte,' I managed to croak, impressed that I had remembered to say please to the moustachioed leader of the Third Reich.

Hitler, nonplussed, simply handed us the two cans and barked the ultimatum (or should I say price?) to us. We paid up and hurried back to our bench. We sat in silence as we gingerly sipped at our cans, imagining strange tastes and smells to be coming from them.

The timetable afforded little choice in the matter of which train we should catch. Though it showed several trains leaving Graz that evening bound for destinations such as Zagreb, all of them had been either scored through with a red pen or their entries covered with white tape. At this point, more sensible travellers may have taken the hint that Yugoslavia was not a popular destination, but the adversity we were faced with only stiffened our foolish resolve to go. We settled for a train that left at 19:02 with the destination of Spielfeld-Straß. Inspection of the map revealed that this hitherto unknown place was right on the border with Austria and what is now Slovenia. We decided that once we arrived at Spielfeld, we would bodge our way into Yugoslavia using local trains until we reached a larger city.

★

Spielfeld-Straß was not a place one would make a special effort to visit. This is not to say that it was unpleasant to look at or that it left a pong in one's nostrils; rather that due to the 'civil' war in Yugoslavia this tiny town had rendered the station a terminus as no traffic was proceeding beyond it. This revelation left us disheartened and angry – partially at our own naivety and partly because we reckoned that someone could have made the effort to mention this to us. We studied the timetable carefully, vainly hoping that we had made a mistake and that at any moment, a large, fast and empty train would arrive and spirit us away to Yugoslavia. We were wrong, of course. At this point, more rational individuals may have sensibly opted to return to Graz and its Nazi beverage salesmen but then we were not rational. Somehow, we had convinced ourselves of an undeniable requirement to visit the war-torn region and the fact that the infrastructure to get us there had failed was not going to be allowed to impede our progress.

The crickets chirped annoyingly loudly on the other side of the tracks. The air hung heavily around us and mosquitoes or other invisible airborne insects strafed our faces and made repeated efforts to fly into our aural canals. Stewart sighed loudly.

'We could walk?' he suggested. On a previous Inter-Rail expedition he had made a similar recommendation which had not been well-received though he obviously thought sufficient time had passed to attempt another such proposal. The idea did not appeal to me in the slightest. The insects were irritating me, I was tired, I reeked – not that I could tell, but I could only vaguely remember the last time I had properly washed myself – and the insides of my thighs had become so hot and sweaty they had started to abrade my testicles. The thought of walking appalled me. Of course, suggesting that my weakened physical state might be a reason for staying in Austria would have been a tacit admission to being a complete girl.

'We could indeed,' I agreed. 'Which way is it? I don't suppose it would be very clever to walk along the tracks.'

Stewart assured me that he knew which general direction to head in and, having persuaded ourselves that it was probably only about two miles to the border, we set off.

★

Walking was generally something we tried to avoid at all costs. It was tiring, it was boring and it was the slowest way imaginable of getting from A to B. We walked along the side of an almost deserted dual-carriageway. Occasionally, rumbling juggernauts would clatter by leaving a stench of exhaust fumes and a cloud of dust. I began to curse myself for ever undertaking such a stupid venture. I was secretly hoping that Stewart would spontaneously declare that he had had enough and that we could simply catch a train back to Vienna and be done with it. That way, the whole thing would be over and I wouldn't lose face.

'I can see the border post,' declared Stewart inaccurately. We peered into the twilight and through the almost impenetrable airborne cocktail of mosquitoes and diesel particulates. What Stewart thought was a border post turned out to be a 24 Hour shop. On reaching it we peered through the window. It seemed to sell only sacks of coffee beans and a variety of bottles, contents unknown. Unimpressed, we continued in the direction we assumed to be south.

My testicles were now protesting in the strongest possible terms that their working conditions (i.e. damp, hot and smelly boxer shorts) were intolerable. This protest took the form of an acute soreness, similar to a complaint known as 'Chef's Arse' which afflicts thousands of kitchen staff the world over. I tried rearranging them to ease the discomfort but I could find no point at which they were not rubbing painfully against one part or other of my anatomy. I decided to carry them in my hands. I didn't care if anyone saw me – I had decided that I would never return to this place and that I couldn't give a fuck what any passing motorist might think. Stewart marched on ahead. I stumbled behind him; my rucksack rubbing on my back, my bollocks in one hand and my guitar in the other. It must have been a pitiful sight. I briefly recalled some Wilfred Owen war poetry we had had to learn at school – 'Bent double, like beggars under sacks'. As far as I was concerned it captured the moment perfectly though I'm sure that veterans of the Great War would, quite justifiably, take exception to me drawing a parallel to my gonad problem with life at the Somme.

After what seemed an age we were able to make out a white sign on the side of the road. It read 'Slovejnia'. Ignorant of the exact location of the war we began to kack ourselves a bit.

We arrived at the sign and, as proof to our mates that we had been as hard as to enter a war-zone, we each posed for a photograph by the sign, holding our guitars as if they were rifles. The disinterested border guards standing in their hut merely flicked their eyes in the direction of our passports as we walked across the border, apparently deciding that the fact that we had passports met the entry requirements for their country. This was not good – we still needed proof of our daring mission.

I presented my passport to the guard once more, this time miming the action one would make when stamping a document. The guard looked at his colleague in a partly bored, partly contemptuous way before reluctantly rummaging under a pile of confiscated cigarettes they were busy smoking to retrieve the stamp. After a short discussion with his mate he changed the date on his stamp. With a short thump of the rubber stamp we had the evidence we needed to impress our disbelieving peers on our return – assuming we weren't killed by shrapnel. I decided to disregard this last thought.

The road was empty, desolate. There were no houses nearby, very few lights across the distant, dark hills, no cars drove past, and no trains were using the railway adjacent to the road. We were now within the former Yugoslav Republic, and we knew there was a war around here somewhere. It might have been miles away, it might have been yards away. Snipers might have been lurking behind trees or in haystacks. It was a strange feeling, knowing that if we were close to the war zone it was possible that someone might attack at any moment. In order to boost morale, therefore, we once again held our guitars across our fronts as if they were rifles, and sang 'Who do you think you are kidding Mr Hitler?' loudly into the still night.

We reckoned, or at least hoped, that the first Slovenian station would be a similar distance from the border to its Austrian counterpart. Filled with optimism, bravado and ignorance we forged ahead. We had passed signs for a place called Maribor which was some 11 miles away.

213

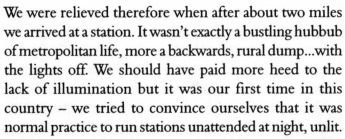

We were relieved therefore when after about two miles we arrived at a station. It wasn't exactly a bustling hubbub of metropolitan life, more a backwards, rural dump...with the lights off. We should have paid more heed to the lack of illumination but it was our first time in this country – we tried to convince ourselves that it was normal practice to run stations unattended at night, unlit.

We tried to decipher the stained and wilting timetable, framed behind a sheet of perspex that was almost opaque with filth. Our little Maglite did its best to penetrate to the necessary information, but it was to no avail. We couldn't read the Cyrillic alphabet.

'I can't believe we didn't foresee this!' sighed Stewart, annoyed at our recurring naivety.

'I reckon we should wait here for a bit,' I suggested unconvincingly. 'There will probably be a train through in the next hour and, providing it's coming from that way,' I pointed back to Austria, 'then we should be OK.'

Neither of us held out much hope of there being a train but we sat there just the same. I don't think we waited even half an hour before our patience was exhausted. We concluded that the station was indeed shut, that there would probably not be any trains in the morning judging by the hitherto unnoticed weeds growing around the tracks and that we should never have set off on such a foolhardy venture. We accepted that we should return to Spielfeld and wait for a train heading in the general direction of civilisation. This idea was met with a mixture of relief that we were now less likely to be ethnically cleansed and reluctance that we had to repeat the sweaty, sooty route along the dual carriageway. It was also demoralising and slightly embarrassing that we had been forced to abort our 'brave' and foolhardy expedition at such an early stage.

When we arrived back at Spielfeld I could barely waddle, let alone walk, such was the condition of my knackers. We were heartened, however, to discover the impending arrival of a train whose destination was civilisation or, more precisely, Vienna Südbahnhof. The term 'impending' is not strictly accurate in this case. By the time we arrived back at Spielfeld's shack of a station it was about 23:30 on Thursday evening: the rescue train wasn't due until 03:47 on Friday morning. We elected to get some sleep but we were also wary that we may oversleep and miss the train or, worse still, fall victim to a roving gang of ruthless, thieving, Yugoslavian gippos.

With this in mind I volunteered to keep first watch while Stewart got some shut-eye. Poo stretched out on a conveniently situated bench and wriggled into his sleeping bag. I took up position on an equally convenient lump of stony soil opposite him. I found it difficult not nodding off myself. After a few minutes I realised I would have to occupy my mind to avoid catastrophe. I decided to try to get to grips with the general concept of polar second moment of area again. Back at home I had experienced extreme difficulty with this engineering principle. This was partly due to our Iranian lecturer's inability to explain anything without following it up with 'Errybowdy unnerstann? Say yayss!' and partly due to the fact that this theory was rock hard. My housemate,

Pearl, concluded that second moment of area was, in fact, a special kind of engineering magic and that it need not be understood but merely accepted. I decided to agree with him and I started translating the posters on the station walls from German. Insurance – boring. Bathroom suites – ditto. Vaginal thrush treatment – shudder. Spiders as gifts – hmmmmm. Maybe I misunderstood that one. I tried again. No, I was right. The general gist was about spiders – there was even a picture of one on the poster. I was right - there were spiders around and they were 'giftig'. That must have something to do with present-giving. I vaguely remembered the word 'giftstoff' from my German lessons.

I sat back, perplexed. The light of realisation slowly grew from a faint glimmer to a bright torch. Giftig meant poisonous. Of course it did; I'd seen it written on canisters of Zyklon B in documentaries on the Discovery Channel. My eyes wandered around in search of a new linguistic challenge. Finding nothing they settled on the area of roof above where Stewart was now soundly asleep. The whole roof was teeming with spiders. Suddenly, a tidal wave of shock and fear overwhelmed me. I jumped up and brushed off my legs and arse in a frenzy, sweeping the invisible (and probably non-existent) arachnids onto the ground. I rushed over and shook Stewart until he woke up. We spent the remaining time pacing up and down the platform, nervously glancing at our legs and each other's backs to ensure we were not about to be attacked.

Thinking about it now I feel a fool. There was some more text below it in a smaller typeface. This probably said something along the lines of 'Come and see these terrifying and lethal predators at Graz Zoo'. I'll never know what was written there now.

– I Will Not Buy This
Record – It Is Scratched –

PAUL

Zombiefied from sleep deprivation, we clumsily made our way at Vienna station to the Budapest train, which at 08:03 began its journey to Hungary.

Although Hungary, along with its erstwhile communist neighbours, was now ostensibly a capitalist state, the view through the grimy windows of the train did little to support this claim. Rows of dilapidated factories and disused buildings covered in a nondescript brown filth lined the track. Luckily this was in the early nineties and the 'grunge' look was 'in' but I knew it wouldn't last. Still, I reassured myself, the outskirts of Sunderland viewed from a train window made one feel as if one was entering Satan's Arse Cleft whereas the town itself, er, was Satan's Arse. Bollocks. The station, when we finally arrived in it, was really rather grandiose and not at all what the approach to Satan's Arse had led us to expect. The ceilings were high above, not only in the platform areas but also in the booking office and general concourse. Plenty of gold Cyrillic writing ran in a line around the walls though we had no idea what it meant. And, even though this was a nation in which our education had led us to expect it was normal to queue for a week to buy a newspaper, there were no queues for the ticket desks.

The thin emulsion of grandeur faded away to nothing as we dawdled down the steps of the imposing station. Although railway stations all over Europe and, probably, the world, do attract the most under-privileged elements of society, I was in no way prepared for the sight that awaited us. In front of us was a huddle of people who were so filthy they had either never seen a bath ever or they'd come out Inter-Railing a few months earlier then lost their tickets. Some of them were exhibiting nervous twitches and perpetually nodding while babbling to themselves, like a late night debate in the House of Lords. To our right was a person of indeterminate gender with no legs, perched on a skateboard. The person looked at us hopefully. Having no money at all we dodged past. A few yards on from the unfortunates we turned around to look at the rest of the attendant crowd. Against the iron railings rested a couple of mattresses. They were the same colour as the people that surrounded them and a cloud of flies relentlessly swarmed over the piss-soaked bedding. Finally there was a bear. The poor animal was obviously in distress and its owner kept it under control by repeated yanks on a chain that was attached to a ring through the bear's nose. Call me a girl but I almost cried at the plight of these people. Sure, I had seen worse things on television like the famines in Africa and the famous footage of that naked Vietnamese girl covered in napalm burns and running down the road but, despite the fact that the content of those broadcast images was more horrific than what I was now witnessing, the sight in front of Budapest station was more shocking as it was, very suddenly, infinitely more real.

Relying on our middle-class upbringings we were able to ignore the plight of other people while concentrating on our own welfare and, as it was lunchtime, we set off

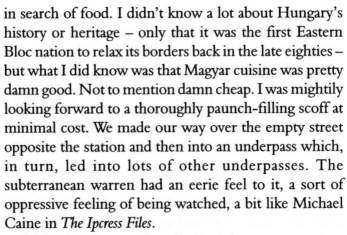

in search of food. I didn't know a lot about Hungary's history or heritage – only that it was the first Eastern Bloc nation to relax its borders back in the late eighties – but what I did know was that Magyar cuisine was pretty damn good. Not to mention damn cheap. I was mightily looking forward to a thoroughly paunch-filling scoff at minimal cost. We made our way over the empty street opposite the station and then into an underpass which, in turn, led into lots of other underpasses. The subterranean warren had an eerie feel to it, a sort of oppressive feeling of being watched, a bit like Michael Caine in *The Ipcress Files*.

Michael Caine, incidentally, is cool.

Stewart and I discussed the possibility of the presence of now obsolete watching and listening devices secreted in the nooks and crannies of this system of walkways – a system that would have allowed a hierarchy of malevolent hypocrites to keep tabs on their hungry, shabbily-dressed, proletarian population. It was a fascinating discussion but unfortunately it did nothing to subdue our growing appetites.

It was a Sunday which, it seemed, meant that even fewer establishments than usual were open for business in Budapest. We walked for about a mile in one direction that hinted that it would turn into a busy commercial area, but failed to live up to its promises and eventually led to another run down and dirty collection of concrete buildings. It was a hot day yet it was also faintly misty and this made us sweat more than even Inter-Railers found acceptable. Eventually we decided that our continuing searches for anything that resembled a cashpoint, a bank or even a restaurant were going to prove fruitless. We resolved to go from Budapest to Prague which, according to our Thomas Cook timetable, would require catching a train from the other side of the city later that afternoon.

The timetable had a map of Budapest the size of a matchbox and it was on this that we depended for finding our way to Nuygati station. The map showed three distinct black blobs (representing railway stations) on a larger, less distinct, grey blob which represented the city. Or should I say cities? One thing I learned that day was that Budapest was formed from two communities situated on either side of the river Danube: one called Buda, the other called Pest. (See, this book isn't just puerile, opinionated profanity – it's also educational, albeit in minuscule amounts.) One thing became certain when looking at this map: with three unnamed roads and an anonymous river shown on it, it wasn't going to be a lot of help in finding our destination. Finally we decided to head in generally the right direction until we saw some road signs which, though we thought we would not be able to read them, we were confident would be obvious in their representation of a station. With 'sort of north-ish' chosen as our desired direction and 'roughly west-ish' ascertained by the position of the sun relative to the time of day, we set off on our quest.

Some readers could be understandably forgiven for assuming that this method of navigation would inevitably fail. However, everyone gets a bit of luck now and again and today we were lucky. Admittedly, it took us about three hours of walking to reach our destination but we felt a profound sense of achievement when we finally did arrive. During our walk, the mist had cleared which had allowed the temperature to soar. On the way we had passed an LED display telling us not only that it was significantly later than lunchtime but also that the temperature was 35 degrees (that's 95 degrees in old money). This sort of weather did nothing for our overall aroma as one can appreciate.

Budapest's Nuygati station was even better appointed than the previous one: it even had an en-suite McDonald's. McBurgers cannot be procured, however, without a supply of money so we were equally impressed to find a Bureau de Change as well.

In front of the grubby grille of the exchange it occurred to us that neither of us spoke a word of Hungarian – well almost, but we'll come onto that later – so we wondered how we should go about communicating. While we were procrastinating over our linguistic shortcomings, an obese tourist in obscenely garish apparel pushed in and demanded to change 'these dollars for some local currency, damn it!' We concluded that English, no matter how bastardised, was spoken in these parts – at least at a Bureau de Change. Before we had left England, my father had fished through his mysterious yellow purse of foreign monies – foreign cash he had acquired over thirty-five years of geographically diverse business trips – and had given me a couple of bank notes, saying,

'If you're going to Eastern Europe you ought to take some exchangeable currency.'

With that he had given me two bank notes: a ten US dollar bill and ten Swiss Francs which I had stuffed into my wallet where I expected them to stay for the duration of our trip. However, since it transpired that the bureau would not give us a cash advance on Stewart's dangerously overloaded Visa card we had no choice but to exchange the two notes.

'How much have we got then?' asked Stewart after the deed had been done. I hastily counted the alien currency. It took about a minute.

'Er, about one thousand, six hundred. Roughly.'

'One thousand, six hundred what?'

'Forints. Is that what these things are or is it the name of the geezer on the note?'

Having established that we were currently 0.16% millionaires, we set off around the station to see what our new found wealth would bring. First stop, obviously, would have to be that bastion of local cuisine, McDonald's. We each had a typically modest repast comprising a couple of burgers, a similar number of portions of French fries, and a doughnut to round off.

'What's left after that little lot?' asked Stewart.

'About fourteen hundred,' I replied. Realising that we had a lot more spending to do before we were rid of a currency that was of no use anywhere else on Earth we ventured outside the station and bought some postcards and stamps from a Budapest barrow boy. The cards made us curious. On them were pictures of beautiful views, splendid palaces and well kept parks: in other words, nothing bearing the remotest resemblance to what we had seen. I wrote one out to my granny and I can remember exactly what I said: 'Dear Granny, here we are in Budapest. I don't know what this place on the front is or even if it is actually in Budapest. This place is a dump – don't believe the postcard. Love Paul. P.S. It is dirt cheap, though.' As I look through reference material now to jog my memory of Budapest I can see the same buildings and parks, and all the write-ups mention superb architecture and tree-lined boulevards, so I can only conclude that Stewart and I somehow contrived to take a route from one side of the city to the other that bypassed every thing of beauty en route. On the other hand, I live in Portsmouth and I expect that if one were to read some travel bumf about it that it would probably emphasise the views of the Solent, the historic naval heritage and the birthplace of Charles Dickens while conveniently forgetting to mention ankle deep litter, endemic crime and the hordes of slappers who wander the city with skirts so short you can see their gussets protruding below the hem. Still, unless I go back to Budapest I shall never know.

After the acquisition of several postcards and stamps we still had more than a thousand Forints. We just couldn't get rid of the stuff. As everything appeared to be so cheap I decided that Hungary was probably a good place to stock up on fags for the rest of the trip. (Those of you who think that there is a Monty Python reference to Hungarians and tobacconists will have to wait until later in the chapter.) My chosen forms of developing lung cancer (allegedly), Marlboro and Camel, were hideously expensive. I could have just about bought three packs and had no change left over so I foolishly decided to try some of the local stuff – second rate imitations of famous American brands called *Denver*, *Route 66* and *Super Mild*. I opted for something that didn't purport to be an American brand and whose name I have forgotten . . . thankfully, as the foul taste of those cigarettes I can still remember today.

★

Back at the station we used the McDonald's subterranean toilet facilities in a attempt to make ourselves feel a little less cooty. As the bogs were so deserted I decided to have a wet shave there, too, as it was the only place in the last few days to have hot running water. The station also had a shop selling useful stuff like tea-towels, decks of cards, boiled sweets and pornography, but the most interesting thing about it was its extensive range of alcohol.

'What do you reckon, Stewart? Vodka or gin?' I asked.

'There's no contest – who dares gins!'

We also bought a bottle of tonic water to make our purchase complete and, as it was such a pleasantly hot afternoon, we took our booze outside to drink it on the steps of a nearby statue.

After our first round Stewart drew my attention to a girl, sitting on her own opposite the statue.

'She wants it,' he suggested with typical subtlety.

'Wants what?'

'It! You know? I think you're in!'

'I doubt it, mate.'

'No, trust me, she fancies you. It's just she hasn't twigged that you're a bassist.'

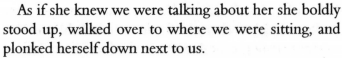

As if she knew we were talking about her she boldly stood up, walked over to where we were sitting, and plonked herself down next to us.

'Are you English?' she asked. We'd been rumbled already.

'Er, yes,' replied Stewart on my behalf. '. . . and you are?'

'I'm from Sweden and I go to school in Paris.'

Not only was this girl typically Swedish in looks, but she was very amicable and totally fluent in English. We shared our gin with her while pointing out that we considered it to be somewhat dangerous to travel alone if one was female. She wasn't bothered though – she seemed to have been all over the place and come off better than we would have in the same circumstances. She was also very modest – while she initially claimed to know a little English she was totally fluent and while she mentioned that she went to school in France she was, in fact, attending the Sorbonne. Why she would want to hang out with us, apart from for scientific interest, was beyond us but we weren't complaining. As we were all going to Prague at half past five that afternoon we agreed to travel together.

Karina, that was her name, wandered off after a bit to get something to read – no doubt she was also fluent in Hungarian – and came back a little while later with a group of Swedish lads that she had bumped into. They too were very agreeable types and we sat around chatting in English while they smoked my dodgy cigarettes for me. It was another one of those moments when you feel embarrassed and ashamed that you are surrounded by a group of foreigners in a foreign country and the conversation's lowest common denominator is English. It seems that most Europeans have a better understanding of foreign languages than we do and I think that's rather sad. What's really sad, though, is that they've learned it from MTV.

A little later still we were approached by a short, squat man in his early forties. He was sweaty and repulsive and was wearing his polyester shirt unbuttoned to the waist. Having been foolish enough to make eye-contact with him, he approached me and began babbling in Hungarian. I looked back at him with a facial expression that I hoped said something like 'Fuck off. I don't understand a word you're saying.'

'You've scored again,' said Stewart helpfully.

'Blah blah blah!' said the little Hungarian. I tried communicating back in English, French and German but it was no good: what I needed was one of those hailing frequency things that they use in *Star Trek* but, accepting my chronological slot was the late twentieth century, I had to go without. He was getting a bit edgy and frustrated now, as if he thought I was feigning my inability to understand him. He produced a wad of bank notes from his pocket and waved them at me. I was getting a bit worried by this point and a Swedish voice sounded out behind me,

'He wants to fuck you. Ha ha ha.'

'Yes, ha ha indeed,' I thought.

'Give him your Hungarian phrase,' urged Stewart.

He was, of course, referring to the famous Monty Python sketch where a Hungarian enters a tobacconist

227

in England and uses a phrasebook to order some fags and a box of matches but the Hungarian phrases are translated by English ones like 'please fondle my buttocks'. Eventually, the exasperated shopkeeper takes the book and reads what he thinks is the Hungarian phrase for 'that's three shillings and sixpence' except the Hungarian phrase was sufficiently insulting for the Hungarian bloke to deck him.

'Yendalavarsey grigenwy stravenka!' I said to the greasy peasant. He paused for a moment, probably aware that what I had just said was not English but realising it wasn't Hungarian either he continued wittering on inanely.

'If I said you had a beautiful body would you hold it against me? I am no longer infected,' giggled one of the Swedes.

'My nipples explode with delight!' added another. The undoubtedly affluent but smelly diminutive homosexual who was trying to proposition me gave up. He looked at me as if to say 'it's your loss', flourished his wad of Forints and wandered off towards McDonald's. Bloody weirdo.

Just before we left on the 23:50 train to Prague, we had time to throw a little money away. We 'impressed' Karina with puerile antics like gaffa-taping coins to the ground and attaching bank notes to a cotton thread while dragging them away from hapless travellers. She was obviously overawed by the occasion as she didn't say a word.

– Fountain Of Feculence –

Paul

Prague was one of the few places I knew a reasonable bit about before I arrived. From what I did know I decided that I liked Prague, I liked its non-conformist attitude over the years, namely the 'Prague Spring' invasion of 1968 and the fact that some plucky Czech resistance fighters had successfully managed to assassinate Nazi cunt Reichsführer Heydrich using only a dodgy Sten gun, a grenade and a bicycle. I was therefore disappointed when I arrived at Praha Hlavni station to find that it was just like Budapest (only with fewer disease-ridden beggars adorning the place).

'I think we should get some money,' offered Stewart, '. . . on my credit card,' he added for good measure.

'What about Alastair? He'll mack you when you get back.'

'I don't care. I'll mack him back.' With the basic, post-return macking agenda roughly mapped out, Stewart approached a bureau de change, concluded a deal and returned with a fistful of cash.

'What the fuck are these?' I enquired.

'Czech crowns . . . or Korunny to thicko bass-players like yourself.'

'Oh,' I remarked, enlightened, 'how many have we, er, I mean *you* got?'

'About five hundred. Do you want some breakfast?' Karina had become disinterested by our banter and had wandered over to a nearby vending trolley and was

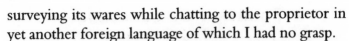

surveying its wares while chatting to the proprietor in yet another foreign language of which I had no grasp.

'How much are the rolls?' Stewart asked Karina.

'Plain rolls cost practically zero Koruna, ones with ham or cheese cost slightly more. I wouldn't touch the ham ones: this stall-holder tells me he gets his meat cheap from a disreputable abattoir.'

'Disreputable abattoir indeed?' said Stewart, taken aback by the extent of this eighteen year old's vocabulary. 'Are there any words they don't teach you at school?'

'Only bloke, knackers, fags, dosh, geezer and ringer. I got them from an on-line slang dictionary on the internet.'

'Ringer?'

'Yes, it's when disreputable car dealers transfer the identity of one car to another to hide its identity.'

'Jesus!' remarked Stewart. Still reeling at our intellectual and linguistic ineffectuality when compared to Karina we bought four cheese rolls, conducting the entire transaction in English.

'How much was that?' I asked, eager to get a feel for what this new currency was worth.

'About thirty pee.'

This had all the makings of a cheap day out.

Though we had decided to go onwards to Berlin later and thence on to Amsterdam, I had decided that I didn't want another cultural jewel, like Budapest, to pass me by, so the plan was to go to Holesovice, the station on the other side of town, ready to catch the train, dump our shit and go back into the city. That was the plan, anyway. Having met with success the day before we

230

decided to go with our rough and ready navigation technique in order to find the station of our departure.

The day was very hot as it had been in Budapest though there was less humidity. We toiled along quiet city streets, foolishly listening to Karina who said she knew Prague. A bit. After about an hour we had become pissed off with the endless trudging and opted to attempt to get a train across the city from the next station we came upon, assuming of course that the next station was not Holesovice. Before too long we found a station called Praha Bubny and when I say 'station' I mean it in its broadest sense. This 'station' was far and away the biggest rail-related dump I ever had the misfortune to set eyes upon. It was made from drab concrete which had become stained by the acid rain of the preceding years and by the sooty excrescence of the exhausts of the Ladas and Trabants which littered the city. The outside of the station wasn't much better. The whole place smacked of the stereotypical image of the Eastern Bloc countries. The only thing I can say about it in its favour is that it reminded me of Michael Caine again and this is 'a good thing'. Karina ventured to the ticket desk which, on closer inspection, turned out to be closed.

'Mind the shit!' shouted Stewart as Karina narrowly avoided a pile of human shite and tissues which some thoughtful soul had left in the middle of the station lobby.

'I can't believe someone took a shit right in the middle of this room,' I said.

'Well, Bubny has to be good for something: it's not much cop as a station,' explained Stewart.

After Bubny we gave up on our plan to catch another train and consigned ourselves to walking the rest of the way. I'm glad we did because the views got better and the streets became less litter-strewn as we progressed. I was particularly impressed with a scrapyard we passed that was full of Second World War tanks and other armoured vehicles. Stewart and Karina humoured me for about five minutes as I stared in wide-eyed longing and wondered if they would take Stewart's Visa card for one of their half-tracks.

'Come on,' urged Stewart, 'you can see those on TV when we get home.'

'But they've got an SdKfz251/16!' I protested weakly.

'God! You're so anal!' he retorted. 'Anal'(ly retentive) was Stewart's word of the moment.

'But it's got flame-throwers and everything . . .'

★

On arrival at Holesovice, Stewart declared that he was not going to walk back into town but that he was going to spend the day sitting, on his own, in the station. I thought he was mad at the time but, on reflection, he may have been removing himself from the frame in the hope that I would hit it off with Karina. He should have known better: I've always been hopeless at that sort of thing. Still, it was his loss and I was not going to miss out on another city.

Unimpaired by the bulk of our rucksacks (and guitar in my case) Karina and I set off back to where we hoped the action would be. It is at this point that I must confess to having done something really studenty and affected: I, or rather we, decided to walk around barefoot as it

232

was such a pleasant day. While this would obviously have been a perfectly reasonable thing to do had we been on a beach in Antigua it was not very clever in a capital city whose streets, like all other cities, were beset by such hazards as broken glass, gravel and shit from a wide range of animals. Still, we carried on regardless, occasionally stopping to bathe our feet in any convenient fountain we chanced upon.

After many minutes of wandering during which we had to circumnavigate a dead cat on the pavement, we arrived at Wenceslas Square – the tourist centre of Prague. I was parched at this point from all the walking I had done and made a bee-line for a nearby drinks vendor (hoping that it wasn't another incarnation of Hitler). I bought a can of beer for thirty-eight pence and sat on a bench to drink it where I reflected upon how much I would have had to pay had I bought this at, say, Piccadilly Circus, the Eiffel Tower or the Spanish Steps. A fortune, I'm sure, and it wouldn't even have been cold, no doubt. The time we were in Prague was the beginning of its resurgence as a popular tourist resort following the fall of Communism with fat western Europeans like us and, worse still, even fatter Americans. Among the cafés selling cups of coffee for the price of a twig and the street artists and traders were Gucci and Dolce & Gabbana boutiques which looked strangely out of place. I felt sorry for the inhabitants of Prague. They'd had to endure the Nazis, then the Commies, and now their city was being transformed by wonderful market forces, about which they could only dream during the Cold War, to a place in which they could no longer afford to live. (That is an

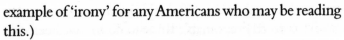

example of 'irony' for any Americans who may be reading this.)

We considered visiting the Franz Kafka museum but Karina managed to talk me out of it by delivering a potted biography of the great man (or whatever he was) on the spot. I thought it was odd that on his deathbed he asked that all of his work be burned. I'd be more concerned about making sure my pornography collection was incinerated.

A while later we stopped to bathe our feet in another fountain. The water in it looked a bit soup-like but plenty of other people were cooling off in it so we dipped our extremities into the water and luxuriated in the sensation of billions of other people's foot bacteria migrating from host to host. The fountain wasn't very big and the jet of water in the centre was just about reachable from the edge. I prepared my groovy Sigg water bottle to receive a fresh charge from what I assumed was a fresh supply of water spurting in the middle of the fountain. As my outstretched arm was almost in range a large hairy hand grasped my forearm. Thinking that I was being mugged I panicked – not too much I hoped, as I was in the presence of a girl and panicking was just not British. I turned to face my would-be attacker to see a large, red-faced Czech beaming from ear to ear. He pointed to my water bottle, then to the fountain and shook his head disapprovingly. Message understood. I wished that I knew how to say 'thank you' in his language but the closest I would have been able to manage was German which, on reflection, might not have been very tactful. I smiled appreciatively at the local who had saved me from drinking from the fountain of feculence.

It was getting late in the afternoon and I wondered how Stewart might be amusing himself on his patch of filthy concrete back at the station. He'd probably be OK: he'd done this sort of thing before. He was probably writing poems that didn't rhyme. Or make sense. In fact he'd been writing such shite for eight years or so and his so-called poems hadn't improved over that period. Still, like most poets, I expect his work won't be worth anything until he dies which is why I have kept some of his original work as an investment.

★

Karina, probably having had a bellyful of us by now, had decided to go to Brno in central Czechoslovakia. We said our goodbyes, did the obligatory yet pointless swapping of addresses and went our separate ways. I'd enjoyed my time with her but the burden of having to act grown-up had been lifted from my shoulders.

'Where to then, Stewart?'

'I've looked at the timetables and the only route with any regular sort of service going in approximately the right direction is to, and you're not going to like this, Berlin!'

I'd never been to Berlin and, despite its groovy and fashionable reputation, I didn't really want to either. Still, if it meant that we had to revisit the Fatherland as a means to going somewhere better, like Holland, then I couldn't really complain.

STEWART

I dozed only lightly after Prague. We were headed towards Amsterdam, via Berlin, which was such an insanely long way that I tried to maintain a state of semi-consciousness to ease the boredom. There was a noticeable jolt, however, as the train ran over an eastern European goat, and as I opened my eyes I could see a vast, blurred, endless shape moving along the corridor. Then he entered the compartment.

'Do you know where we are?' Paul asked, sitting down.

'I hope we're back in the free world again.'

'Well, I just saw the sign for Dresden, so we're back in the Fatherland.'

'Dresden, eh?' I whispered. 'As twinned with Coventry in 1944?'

I looked outside at this famous place, eager to spot the plethora of concrete that had been the utilitarians' attempt to make everyone as depressed in their daily lives as possible, thereby giving an economic boost to the fragile clown industry.

Suddenly, without warning, I spotted a nineteenth century house.

'Oops,' I said, 'looks like we missed a bit.'

★

Berlin was the only city in the world of which I possessed a piece before visiting it. The wall came down while I was studying hard at university. The same day, in fact. I immediately hatched a plan to take myself and six other students (in order to share costs) to Berlin in a 1968 Morris Minor with dodgy brakes. We were to carry a

236

hammer and chisel on the way out, and to return with a boot full of historic rubble. Despite the flawlessness of this plan and the initial eagerness of all concerned, it all fizzled and floundered. Just like an earlier scheme I had hatched to rescue Terry Waite from Beirut using a Land Rover and a very powerful torch. So, pushed on by boundless student apathy, we remained in the bar and watched other students demolish the wall in the name of Freedom and Late Opening everywhere.

Some days later, however, I received a letter from MG Julie in Germany. MG Julie drove an MGB roadster, hence the name. Although the car shared many of its vital component parts with those in my Morris Minor, such as the bonnet catch and the dipstick, it was always viewed with more wide-eyed wonder by students in the bus queue than was my vehicle. MG Julie was serving time at a German university as part of her course, and sellotaped to her letter was a tiny fragment of the wall.

Thus I was familiarised with part of the city long before my nocturnal arrival, though what I eventually saw as we pulled into the station bore no resemblance whatever to the portion of brick dust in my letter. In fact the two girls I was gawping at so intently looked more like movie stars than rubble. They were standing in the corridor next to our compartment, kitted out for Inter-Rail with full rucksacks and captivating smiles.

'I think we should get off here,' I suggested to Paul.

'Why?' he asked, looking out of the window at ruin, deprivation and scum (there was quite a strong reflection in the glass).

'I've never been to Berlin,' I explained.

'But you're here now. Why spoil it by getting off the train? It's nearly eleven – we could be stuck here all night.'

'That's why,' I said, pointing at the two Dutch Inter-Railers who were weaving such magic over me by completely ignoring me.

'They've probably got somewhere to stay. Hitler's bunker or a burned-out tank.'

'So we'll have to stay with them. I'll go and ask if they'd mind us sleeping with them.'

I opened the door to the corridor and looked at the girls.

'Are you girls getting off here?'

'Yes. Would you like to sleep with us?'

'That would be just dandy.'

Having rehearsed this conversation in my head, it was time to speak to them.

'Are you girls getting off here?' I asked, pointlessly preparing myself for the best possible reply.

'Yes. But we have nowhere to sleep. Do you know where there is a hostel?'

'There's one in Eastbourne,' I replied, unhelpfully.

'I'm sorry?'

'I'm Poo, by the way,' I told them, 'and this is Paul, but he's a bass-player.'

'Oh,' they replied in unison, not quite sure to what to make of this revelation.

'I'm Myra,' said the tall, blonde and stunningly attractive one, 'and this is Kyra'. She pointed at her shorter, but equally attractive friend. 'Don't laugh will you?'

'About what?'

'Our names. Myra and Kyra. People think we're joking.' Paul and I were used to this, though. We'd met two Dutch girls in Castellane one year called Marianne and Marion and we'd also met another two in Italy both called Inge. In fact it seemed the norm rather than any phenomenon that similarly named Dutch girls should travel Europe together.

'Why don't we go and look for a hostel together?' asked Myra.

Invitations like that grew on trees about as often as recognisable melodies came out of Paul's guitar.

'An excellent idea,' I replied.

'You get off first, girls,' said Paul, putting on his rucksack. 'Mind the goosestep.'

Berlin was dark, damp and quiet that night. The walls of the station were plastered with peeling posters, as if discarded newspapers had been picked up from the ground and glued to the brickwork. The lamplight flickered moodily, shining off the wet road surface, illuminating the scene in black and white like an old James Dean photo.

'I can't see any bunkers from here,' I said, as we stood on the station steps. We looked up and down the street at the silent, shadowy buildings. There was no indication of any hotels or hostels, or even of somewhere at which we could afford to stay.

'I'll ask inside the station if they know where we can stay,' said Myra, disappearing back inside.

Whilst she was gone I dropped my crap against the wall and trotted off to the corner of the street to see what mysteries lurked out of sight. I stood, panting, at the junction and surveyed the landscape. To my left stretched an endless road, closely lined on either side by tall, grey townhouses. To my right was some kind of park behind a high wall. There were no recognisable signs of any description, let alone accommodation. I ran back to the station.

'What's there?' asked Paul.

'Nothing. Not even a Hitler Youth Hostel.'

Myra came back clutching a leaflet.

'This has a list of places where we can stay,' said Myra. 'Most of them are very close to each other. If we walk for about two kilometres we should be able to find somewhere.'

Paul's face twisted into an expression of absolute horror at the prospect. I took a deep breath. There had to be another solution, one that didn't involve walking anywhere.

I tried reasoning with her.

'Walking's shit,' I explained. 'Why don't we get on a train somewhere? We can sleep for free on a train.'

'But we came to see Berlin,' protested Kyra. 'It's the last day of our holiday tomorrow and we wanted to visit it before we go home.'

'Yes, but surely it's not worth the effort of walking anywhere?' said Paul. 'Nothing is.'

'There's another train to Amsterdam in an hour. Let's sleep on that one,' I suggested.

'Come on,' said Paul. 'Otherwise you might walk all night and still not find somewhere.'

The girls held a quick Inter-Rail meeting in Dutch, then announced the decision of the Board.

'OK.'

– EEN DONDEHONDEVONDEROPP –

PAUL

Our escape train from the beloved Fatherland left Berlin Hauptbahnhof at thirteen minutes past midnight with the destination of Amsterdam Centraal. The train was strangely empty for such a route between such major, fashionable cities and we naively hoped that it would stay that way as most passengers would have boarded at the station of origin. With four of us in the compartment designed to take six, we managed to spread our collective crap so as to occupy completely all the remaining space. From our exclusive compartment we watched as various vaguely familiar landmarks passed by the window. The only one I can remember now is the oddly bulbous TV or radio tower and we were busy discussing its lack of architectural merit when we arrived at Berlin Zoo station. Zoo was an apt name in the circumstances: all of the passengers we had expected to see at the Hauptbahnhof were milling around on the crowded platform like wildebeest clambering over each other and pushing in front of one another. The compartment was comfortable with just the four of us in our sleeping bags, but if any strangers butted in things could get unpleasant.

Hundreds of people crammed into the corridors of the train and spread themselves around as we started moving again. The door to our compartment slid open and shut incessantly for the next half an hour as dopey American and Japanese 'Euro-Railers' stuck their heads in, ascertained the fullness of the compartment, and

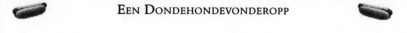

grunted their disappointment before moving on to the next one.

When the interruptions had stopped, the girls asked what we were going to do once we arrived in Amsterdam. The truth of gorging ourselves with cheeseburgers and drugs Elvis-style and then taking in some high quality pornography did not seem an appropriate disclosure so we opted to lie.

'We thought we might see Anne Frank's house and maybe do a museum or something,' I said, trying not to blow my cover. Stewart looked at me in disbelief and then he realised I was trying to appear mature and sophisticated.

'Yeah, and we might do a live sex-show too,' he added, helpfully.

Myra and Kyra looked at each other, deeply unimpressed.

'Only joking,' he squeaked.

It was obvious that we would have to put away our puerile antics for a little while if we were all to arrive at our destination unscathed by one another. It transpired that Myra and Kyra were at university in the city of excesses and inexplicably volunteered to show us around once we arrived. We accepted, naturally.

Once we had arrived at Centraal and dodged the inevitable offers of budget accommodation, budget drugs and budget sex, the girls led us down the main road that runs in a straight line from the station's main doors into town. Our destination was the 4 Jahrten café. I apologise for the spelling, it is from memory and therefore almost

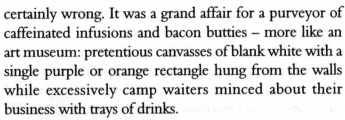

certainly wrong. It was a grand affair for a purveyor of caffeinated infusions and bacon butties – more like an art museum: pretentious canvasses of blank white with a single purple or orange rectangle hung from the walls while excessively camp waiters minced about their business with trays of drinks.

'One of my friends did these paintings,' said Kyra with more pride than was warranted.

'Really?' I muttered as noncommittally as possible, hoping that I would not be required to give a more concrete endorsement of her mate's artistic abilities. We were led through the café and out onto a floating pontoon on one of the many canals. Tables and chairs were arranged neatly, accompanied by sun umbrellas and assorted plants in tubs. It was undoubtedly pleasant but it was becoming more and more apparent that, relative to us, Myra and Kyra were fairly high up the social ladder while we were the wedges at the bottom that stop it slipping. This particular establishment, we decided, was not the sort of place we would have graced with our custom voluntarily.

We examined the minimalist but undoubtedly aesthetically pleasing menu card. My suspicions were confirmed – this was a hoity-toity socialite's café, devoid of bacon sarnies, tomato ketchup and other staple café fodder but endowed with a surfeit of tofu kebabs, falafel and other inedible shite. I managed to find an Emmenthal roll and a cup of tea hidden at the bottom of the menu in the small print like a gastronomic black sheep. A waiter came over to take our order and he started

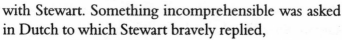
with Stewart. Something incomprehensible was asked in Dutch to which Stewart bravely replied,

'Een dondehondevonderopp.'

Stewart's confidence in his ability to speak Dutch was his alone following an intensive Linguaphone course he had undertaken before we left England on the grounds that it would be useful for chatting up Dutch birds. His plan was fatally flawed by the fact that every Dutch person I have ever met speaks impeccable English. The waiter was no exception.

'Would you like that in granary bread, sir?' Stewart looked distinctly pissed off by the waiter's reaction to his attempt to speak the language but I was not surprised in the least. I'd seen it happen countless times before to countless other people. I'd been in a burger joint in Osnabrück with a language student and on ordering our food the Turkish employee replied with 'Do you want fries with that?' It's demoralising and raises the question of why do we bother to learn a foreign language in the first place? Still, those people who reply in English to remarks made in their own language are doing it to be helpful rather than to undermine your confidence. At least, that's what I like to think. I ordered my stuff in English and when the waiter returned some minutes later he helpfully indicated that he had brought a small jug of milk for my tea as I was English. Myra and Kyra found this amusing and started laying into the way the English take milk in their tea. Feeling that we were already on the pointy end of some of the comments that had been made I was not prepared to lose face any further and

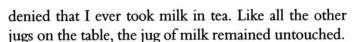

denied that I ever took milk in tea. Like all the other jugs on the table, the jug of milk remained untouched.

We left the 4 Jahrten with the large bill having been paid by our Dutch hosts, to our eternal relief. Myra and Kyra had to catch another train to somewhere that we weren't. Stewart and I said our goodbyes and then had to take the tricky decision between more porn or more drugs. We opted for the latter and made our way to a likely-looking establishment where we decided to carry out the transaction in English to avoid any more put-downs.

'Can I see the card please?' I asked. The hippie behind the counter produced a menu with about a dozen or so pages. On each page was a zip-lock bag containing a sample of the wares being offered and a brief textual description in Dutch, English and German. We plumped for Sinsemilla: a fine variety of marijuana with a high narcotic content. Stewart, despite his previous misgivings, chose a cake and we were on our way, drifting aimlessly about the streets of Amsterdam. Apart from finding a kitchen appliance shop called Smeg which had us in narcotic paroxysms for ages we found little more to entertain us. We had put ourselves in the frame of mind that we were on the homeward stretch of our journey and now our main concern was just getting back. A few hours later, once the grass had worn off, we found ourselves back in McDonald's, stuffing ourselves with a variety of burgers prior to our Paris-bound departure at a quarter past ten.

– THE AROMA OF BELGIUM –

STEWART

The route from Amsterdam down to Paris was like a final sprint after a long, sweaty marathon. Not that I'd know. We would soon be crossing the Channel towards home, where we would have to try to fit back in to our own civilised society, where beards came with moustaches and where you could buy a loaf of bread that would last all week (provided you didn't eat it). In preparation for this cultural re-integration I tried washing myself in the toilet at the end of the compartment, but the trickle of water coming out of the tap wasn't enough to make any impression on my dirt. I stood with one foot on the floor switch and with one hand stuck limpet-like to the grab rail so that I didn't fall over, but it was virtually impossible to initiate effective cleansing. I made do with wiping some of the deposits from my face and returning, no less smelly, to my seat just in time to witness mile upon mile of Belgian allotments. It was early in the morning, and they were wonderful sights to behold: sheds, carrots, potatoes, and black plastic bin-liners.

'If you were to magnify, by about a thousand times,' explained Paul, 'the surface of my arse . . .'

'I thought it already was,' I interjected.

'Let me finish my theory,' he continued. 'If you were to magnify it, and put a photo of it up on the train window here, I bet it wouldn't look any different to those allotments.'

'Why's that? Have you got little Belgians smoking pipes and planting turnips in your crack, then?'

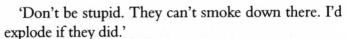

'Don't be stupid. They can't smoke down there. I'd explode if they did.'

After that the conversation started to get a bit silly, so we both simultaneously shut up and started cogitating. I thought about the aroma of Belgium, which was starting to break through all of my nasal defences. Then I thought about Paris, which was frustratingly distant. It didn't seem likely that I would be able to hold my breath until we hit the French border. Still, we had endured much of Europe on this trip, and Europe had endured even more of us, so I reckoned I could just about make it.

What had it all been for, I wondered? I knew I wouldn't have a suntan under the grime I was wearing, and I had definitely spent more than I had budgeted for (which was approximately zero). The only positive result of my travels that I could think of was that I had lost a bit of weight, though that was mostly from my brain.

PAUL

The very last part of our journey passed in a semi hallucinogen-induced haze. It wasn't until we had finally arrived at the supermarket in Le Havre that I realised I had passed through French customs with a zip-lock bag full of grass. Thankfully the border controls in mainland Europe were far slacker than their UK equivalents and my passage from one country to another had not brought about any body cavity searches nor any spell of detention.

In the car park of Continent *hypermarché* we mused on what we should do with the offending bag of herbs. I toyed with the idea of mailing the whole lot back to myself using the name of my old head of sixth form who

I hate. He might have been a right old bastard when at school but I didn't think his despotic conduct warranted a possible police investigation. I decided to smoke the rest and what I couldn't manage, Stewart could eat. We then spent the remainder of our money on a selection of fine French things from the hypermarket: I bought wine and beer, Stewart bought envelopes.

'You wouldn't believe how much cheaper they are in France,' he protested later under cross-examination. I thought he was sad.

The ferry left in the late afternoon. My memory of it is scant due to the intoxicated state I was in at the time, and my desire to recount it now is equally weak due to the beer I have consumed this lunchtime. I think it must have crossed the English Channel, anyway.

When we arrived back in Blighty the sun shone pathetically for August, and the sights and sounds all had a familiarity that removed any hint of the challenge of daily living that we had endured these past weeks. Returning home was an anti-climax – our quest to annoy as many foreigners as we could just fizzled out and stopped in an instant. Stewart chose to return to his Mum's house for a bath and a hot meal of which the main constituent was not mechanically separated meat. I chose to return to my student digs in Scumhampton, just up the road from Portsmouth, which would be deserted during the summer holidays and just right for recuperating in.

Thus our last Inter-Rail adventure had come to its inevitable, grubby conclusion. We'd offended countless people, polluted water-courses, taken advantage of other people's hospitality, helped the ailing European pornography industry, made crass and thoughtless remarks at the expense of the pride of other nations and managed to avoid, yet again, being robbed or sexually interfered with by swarthy foreign homosexuals. For this we were grateful but I couldn't help feeling that we were getting a bit long in the tooth for all this continental capering. If we ever wanted to do it again, chances were we'd need a senior citizen's rail pass.

– Insult-Free Zone –

Here are some free insults:

'You smell.'

'Tosser.'

'You smelly tosser.'

'You smell of toss.'

'You are a scummer.'

Je n'en ai rien à foutre.

'You look like Rodney Dangerfield.'

– Index of Profane Words Liable to Induce Childish Amusement in Mentally Weak Persons –

– ESSENTIAL INTER-RAIL ACCESSORIES –

The Little Book of Essential Foreign Insults

Communicating your superior opinions to Johnny Foreigner can be an uphill struggle at the best of times, but with this essential phrase book you can indulge in derogatory discourse wherever you travel and make sure they get the message.

The Little Book of Essential Foreign Swear Words

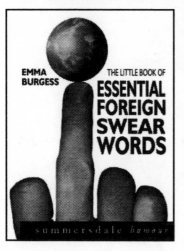

When you go on holiday abroad, it's important to be able to communicate with the natives. It's useful to know, for example, whether the policeman who is trying to bundle you into the back of a van with his truncheon up your arse is calling you a *bastard* or a *cunt*. With this book, you will not only be able to understand him, but you'll also be able to retort in a suitably charming manner.

253

– BY THE SAME AUTHORS –

If you were sufficiently offended by *Don't Mention the War!*, you may be interested in avoiding its illegitimate sister title, *Don't Lean Out of the Window!* by the same authors. It's another 256 pages of Inter-Rail adventures in Europe, with a further cast of completely innocent Europeans who have the piss taken out of them for no reason, plus the usual selection of girls who don't want to get off with the authors and the German homosexuals who do.

To avoid this book, ask your bookseller not to sell you: *Don't Lean Out of the Window!*

More of Stewart Ferris' books can be found on www.stewartferris.com.

'A most entertaining read. Marvellous.' Stephen Fry

Don't lean out of the window!

A European misadventure

Stewart Ferris   Paul Bassett

summersdale *travel*